PRAISE FO~~R URBAN ACES~~

"*Urban ACEs* equips administrators, teachers, and students alike to navigate the challenges of working in and matriculating through an academic system that has typically overlooked the dysfunction found in inner city homes. The scholarly and experiential approach taken by Dr. Matthews in writing this book provides credibility for administrators while remaining relatable to students who have endured adverse childhood experiences."

> —**Charles Daniels Jr.**, Academic Advisor, University of Memphis, Author of *Faith for the Day*

"Here at last an honest and compassionate educator places his head, heart, and hands into practices that will enhance the lives of urban students who are traumatized by adverse childhood experiences. Dr. Matthews has added to the literature an insightful guide for use by school leaders who seek to make a difference in the lives of children of all levels."

> —**Reginald Leon Green**, Former Leadership Department Chair, University of Memphis, Author, *Practicing the Art of Leadership: A Problem Based Approach to Implementing the Professional Standards for Educational Leaders*

"Dr. Matthews has masterfully woven a very powerful, thought-provoking autobiographical sketch rich with education and mental health themes into a practical and informative tapestry of knowledge for educators to better engage in trauma informed care. Undoubtedly, *Urban Aces* adds to the literary examination and analysis in trauma in education and should be required academic reading in universities across the US."

> —**Jason Ingram,** JD, MA, MSW, CEO, Will to Health

"ACEs have been identified, studied, treated, and prescribed antidotal interventions, yes! Dr. Matthews has also created a functional, relatable and strategic road map to reaching, teaching and empowering students to their personal healing from ACEs-related traumas. What an extraordinary tool to champion for students who are subconsciously or diligently seeking their truths. I am inspired and hopeful about the trajectory and future of students, educators, and communities that will benefit from Dr. Matthews' heart work."

—**Erin R. Harrington,** Licensed Master Social Worker, Licensed School Social Worker, Mental Health Professional, Adjunct Professor, University of Memphis, School of Social Work

"Dr. Marcus Matthews' book, *Urban Aces*, provides an outstanding guide for supporting children and youth who are facing traumatic life situations. He has the perfect resume for suggestions he provides, having grown up in a difficult situation in Memphis and finding education as a key to successfully navigating his way into a better situation. Chapters on 'find good friends, develop a strong work ethic, and make a way out of no way' are especially useful guides for teachers, counselors or others who are trying to help these young people. It should be required reading for urban school teachers."

—**Dr. Dan Lattimore,** PhD, Professor, College of Professional and Liberal Studies, Retired Dean, College of Professional and Liberal Studies

"In *Urban ACEs*, Dr. Matthews provided a very detailed and transparent account of his personal traumatic experiences as a child and teen and credits his ability to overcome those environmental obstacles by maximizing the positive education outlets that were available which led to success far above and beyond the adverse experiences that he had once faced."

—**Torrey Singleton,** EdS, Former Principal and Special Education Advocate

"Through his personal and professional reflections, Dr. Matthews is able to connect the reader to the realities surrounding adverse childhood experiences (ACEs) in relation to child academic and social development. This book is highly recommended for educators who are seeking to gain stronger relationships with their students and identify ways to implement a trauma-informed classroom. I thank Dr. Matthews for his transparency by sharing his first-hand experience with trauma as a way to connect the reader to the content. As stated, 'There is no excuse powerful enough to stop your student from doing what they set their heart and mind to do. They simply need your support.' The best way to give that support is by being trauma-informed. Our students need us to show up for them."

—**Moe Nicole** MSW, MEd, Author of *Live Out Loud*

"Dr. Matthews, or Marcus as I know him, takes a brave and undaunted approach of 'exposing' and 'blaming,' usually himself, on his personal journey and the trauma of ACEs. Sharing his personal testimony asserts his credibility and provides a profound and necessary approach to saving our current and future children— giving them a real 'focus' to share. Marcus's story puts an 'F' on ACEs—making every step in support come alive."

—**Dr. Richard Potts,** Director of Instructional Leadership, Christian Brothers University

"With *Urban Aces,* Dr. Matthews has outlined a framework that is effective not just for helping traumatized students. His ten strategies for managing adverse childhood experiences are easy for students and young professionals alike to implement. I recommend this book as an important step in empowering young people, especially new lawyers, to reach their full potential and not be limited by circumstances from their childhood that were beyond their control."

—**Nicole Makeda,** MEd, JD, In-House Corporate Legal Counsel at Nationwide Mutual Insurance Company

"We are not teaching children how to deal with emotions from their past, so they do not have a clue how to journey through their current situations. Dr. Matthews has given us the tools beautifully written in his new book, *Urban ACEs*. Adults spend a lifetime trying to correct what happened in their childhoods, and Matthews presents a blueprint on how to help our children with behavior issues past and present. His book is a must read for parents, mentors or anyone dealing with children. The journey to manhood or womanhood is hard; now it does not have to be 'as hard' because of the tools presented in *Urban ACEs*."

—**Charles E. Williams, Jr.**, Charles Plus Creative/ WEG Media Group

"Urban ACEs is a must read for anyone who is truly committed to the development of students traumatized by ACEs. The author does an excellent job of sharing real life experiences that shaped his life and influenced his development. The 10 points (chapters) shared in his book create an excellent template for districts, administrators and teachers to help students with ACEs develop into productive, contributing individuals in spite of their negative childhood experiences. As the author stated, 'The load is heavy, but the rewards are worthwhile.'"

—**Commodore C. Primous Sr.**, Retired Elementary School Principal, Project Manager, Director, Effective Practice Incentive Community, Memphis City Schools

"Dr. Matthews' testimonies and strategies are poignant and very relatable for urban stakeholders. The release of *Urban ACEs* comes at a perfect time to assist school districts with this issue."

—**Dr. Roderick Richmond**, Executive Director, Student Support Services, Shelby County Schools

"When I first met Marcus Matthews, he was working toward becoming an ace newspaper reporter. A shift in priorities led him to teaching others to write on a university level and, ultimately, to secondary school teaching and administration. Marcus, whose childhood experiences gave him a high ACE score, is one of those people who recognizes opportunity where some see only problems. His vision, experiences and scholarship paved the way for this guidebook. Marcus is an example of overcoming adversity, and this guidebook delineates a path from despair to success."

—**Jim Willis**, Former Editor and President, *Birmingham Post-Herald*

"Finally, the defining work on ACEs that educators in the classroom and lawmakers on Capitol Hill have been awaiting. Dr. Matthews has provided the Swiss Army Knife of ACEs literature that enables educators and advocates to address the unique challenges of building better children from youth who've been emotionally fractured and physically broken by the devastating impacts of the worst environments. I'm better equipped now to create educational opportunities that work for the children burdened by the weight of ACEs."

—**G. A. Hardaway Sr.,** Tennessee State Representative, Chairman, TN Black Caucus of State Legislators, Visionary and Cofounder of the Memphis Academy of Health Sciences Middle and High Schools

"In *Urban ACEs*, Dr. Matthews eloquently offers strategies in addressing students with adverse childhood experiences from a trauma-informed approach. Through the utilization of personal experience, we see a level of sentiment that is critical for educational practitioners when supporting childhood trauma. This is definitely every teacher's must have!"

—**Neshellda Johnson**, Teacher

"I don't know the last time I read a book that made me cry, then turned around and taught me a lesson on how to deal with the problem presented. Working in a Title I school, I see many of the situations mentioned in *Urban ACEs*. I recommend this book for every educator working with students who have experienced trauma or working in an urban school district. *Urban ACEs* also explains the impact an educator can have on a child's life."

—**Casaundra M. Smith**, Assistant Principal, Jefferson County Public Schools

"Dr. Matthews' ability to address the issue of adolescent trauma, its impact and practical ways in which educators can overcome in their classroom is unparalleled. This book is a game changer!"

—**Dr. Patrick Washington,** Executive Director, Man Up Teacher Fellowship

"This unique look into the author's personal life is a fascinating and thoughtful tool to support educators with students who are experiencing similar challenges and provides a roadmap to successfully overcome them."

—**Dr. Bobby White**, Founder/CEO Frayser Community Schools

Urban ACEs

How to Reach and Teach Students Traumatized by
Adverse Childhood Experiences

by Dr. M.L. Matthews

© Copyright 2019 Dr. M.L. Matthews

ISBN 978-1-63393-985-1

All rights reserved. No part of this publication may be reproduced, stored in a retrieval system, or transmitted in any form or by any means—electronic, mechanical, photocopy, recording, or any other—except for brief quotations in printed reviews, without the prior written permission of the author.

Published by

◄ köehlerbooks ™

3705 Shore Drive
Virginia Beach, VA 23451
800–435–4815
www.koehlerbooks.com

URBAN ACES

HOW TO REACH AND TEACH STUDENTS TRAUMATIZED BY ADVERSE CHILDHOOD EXPERIENCES

DR. M.L. MATTHEWS

VIRGINIA BEACH
CAPE CHARLES

TABLE OF CONTENTS

INTRODUCTION...IX

CHAPTER 1..1
DEVELOP A STRONG WORK ETHIC

CHAPTER 2..8
CHOOSE BATTLES WISELY

CHAPTER 3...14
DEVELOP TALENTS

CHAPTER 4...24
KEEP YOUR BEST FOOT FORWARD

CHAPTER 5...29
FIND GOOD FRIENDS

CHAPTER 6...49
MAKE A WAY OUT OF NO WAY

CHAPTER 7...55
FORGIVE

CHAPTER 8...65
EMBRACE DISAPPOINTMENT

CHAPTER 9...75
KEEP YOUR BALANCE

CHAPTER 10..80
BE YOUR BROTHERS' AND SISTERS' KEEPER

CLOSING WORDS...85
ABOUT THE AUTHOR..86

INTRODUCTION

Part of the difficulty of addressing an issue as serious and sensitive as adverse childhood experiences (ACEs), traumatic experiences people have before age eighteen, is that it involves the concepts of "exposing" and "blaming." For example, though I love my mother, father, and three brothers with all my heart, the truth is that domestic violence, parental separation, parental incarceration, parental substance abuse, my older brother's death, and mental illness in my home disrupted my childhood. Because of this, there is no way that I can honestly write this book—my personal account of how I overcame ACEs—without "exposing" and exploring these experiences, which some people may interpret as "blaming."

My intent, however, is not to make my parents or anyone else I love feel as if I've thrown them under the bus. My intent is not to shame my father or embarrass my mother. They have been through enough. No, truly my intent is to help you as an educator, parent, guardian, or other influential adult help children achieve balance after being thrown off kilter. To do that as effectively as possible, I could not sugarcoat what really happened to me in my childhood. The stories that follow come straight from my life growing up in Memphis, Tennessee, attending Shelby County Schools (formerly called the Memphis City Schools), and coping with my own personal ACEs—and these stories are raw. That said, I would like to apologize to my parents here and now for any heartache that I might cause by going back in time to relive certain events. Please know that I love you both deeply and that the point of this project is to help as many people, young and old, as possible.

Before I explain in detail the intent of this book, I want to acknowledge that my father eventually overcame a drug addiction and alcoholism and that he has a healthy relationship with my mother now that they are separated. It also does my heart glad to know that my mother has received treatment and support for her mental illness and is now as satisfied and self-reliant as she has ever been. And while my second oldest brother was murdered decades ago, I still miss him. It hurts not to have him on this earth with me, but I am okay.

In fact, through all that I have seen, experienced, and endured, I am okay. Indeed, I am better than okay. I am successful—as a man, a scholar, an author, a producer, and an educator. Still, with all my personal accomplishments, what makes me happiest is knowing that my family is okay. We have all dealt with trauma, drama, and struggle. We have all endured hardships as soldiers. Though we have hurt each other at times, we have all loved—and still love—each other.

Has this book been difficult for me to write? Yes. But I felt called to do it because helping children overcome ACEs to achieve their own form of success motivates me to no end. While I reflected on my life to write *Urban ACEs: How to Reach and Teach Students Traumatized by Adverse Childhood Experiences*, I came up with ten focus areas: *develop a strong work ethic, choose battles wisely, develop talents, keep your best foot forward, find good friends, make a way out of no way, forgive, embrace disappointment, keep your balance*, and *be your brothers' and sisters' keeper*.

Without even knowing it, throughout my childhood and adulthood, I had adopted these strategies to gain and maintain balance. These ten concepts will serve as the frame around the picture of how we discuss supporting students dealing with adverse childhood experiences.

As you read *Urban ACEs*, you will see that I also speak to some of the concepts presented in *The Trauma-Informed School: A Step-by-Step Implementation Guide for Administrators and School Personnel*. The book, written by Jim Sporleder and Heather T. Forbes, is one that I learned from as the dean at trauma-informed Craigmont Middle School in Memphis; for the uninitiated, a trauma-informed school is one where faculty members have been trained to help traumatized students.

I use a rubric from Sporleder and Forbes' book in my day-to-day duties. It is called "The Five Critical Steps to Implementing a Trauma-Informed School" and involves concepts, mantras, and strategies for helping traumatized youth. As you read *Urban ACEs*, keep the following steps, which come directly from the book, in mind:

1. **CONCEPT:** The stress is coming from outside of school.
   MANTRA: It's not about me.
   STRATEGY: Drop your personal mirror.
2. **CONCEPT:** Allow the student to de-escalate and regulate before solving the issue at hand.
   MANTRA: Problem solving and solutions can't be worked through while "in the moment."
   STRATEGY: Designate a quiet place(s) where students can feel safe to de-escalate.
3. **CONCEPT:** It's never about the issue at hand. It goes much deeper.
   MANTRA: What's really driving this child's behavior?
   STRATEGY: Be the one who listens and values the student's

voice . . . ask how you can help. Explore the underlying issue behind the behavior.

4. **CONCEPT:** It's a brain issue, not a behavioral issue.

MANTRA: My job is to help this student regulate, not simply behave.

STRATEGY: Incorporate regulatory activities into the culture of the classroom and support students in the ability to learn how to self-regulate.

5. **CONCEPT:** Discipline is to teach, not to punish.

MANTRA: Discipline should happen through the context of relationship.

STRATEGY: Use consequences that keep students in school and foster the building of trust and safety with caring adults.

As we journey through *Urban ACEs*, we will explore some of these steps, in addition to my ten strategies, to assist you in helping traumatized children grow and reach their full potential.

Let's begin . . .

Source: *The Trauma-Informed School: A Step-by-Step Implementation Guide for Administrators and School Personnel* by Jim Sporleder and Heather T. Forbes

CHAPTER 1

DEVELOP A STRONG WORK ETHIC

The nature of "work ethic" is grounded in the cliché "Hard work pays off." That saying is most definitely true. In my nearly forty years on this earth, I have not known anyone who has dedicated himself or herself to working toward a goal and not seen results. While I cannot say that every student will attain every desire of their heart just because they try, I can say that if anyone wants to receive the desires of their heart, then hard work is required. A traumatic experience should not keep any individual from being as successful as they want to be.

As an adult supporting a traumatized child, you are helping a young person who might not always be motivated. Sometimes it might take a second for the student to "get things going." As a result, you might need to drop your personal mirror, give the youth some time, listen to what's wrong, use a regulation strategy, and provide a fitting consequence before guiding him or her back to their task. It will take effort, but the results will be plentiful. One of your goals will be to show them why staying on task is critical to achieving goals. The following story from my life shows how having a tireless work ethic led me to positive results. It can be used as an example for your students to show them why it is necessary to engage in hard work to achieve dreams.

VARSITY BASKETBALL

I fantasized about the day I could finally play with the big boys. Watching them run, defend, make shots, and dunk the basketball awed me. The only thing more amazing than watching the pros on television or my older brothers in the backyard was playing the game of basketball with my own friends. Basketball was all I cared about; it was all I thought about. The routine never changed for me—I went to school, I finished my homework, and I watched or played basketball. In the summer, I was in the backyard putting up shots as soon as the sun rose. Basketball helped me relieve stress. When I was about eight years old, it became an outlet to help me navigate troublesome times.

At ten years old, I was the best basketball player in my fifth-grade class. I could have tried to sound humble and say I was "one of the best," but I have the evidence to prove that I was the best in my grade. Back in my time, Westside Elementary School combined a fifth and sixth grade class due to low enrollment and teacher positions. Classes were consolidated and one teacher, Mrs. Clark, ended up with a classroom made up of fifth- and sixth-grade students. I was one of them.

Mrs. Clark's split class consisted of children who were considered capable of performing at a high academic level without as much instructional time as some other students. For example, all the CLUE kids were part of the split class. CLUE stood for Creative Learning in a Unique Environment and was a program for those whose test scores were on the academically gifted level. The split classroom setup was unique. The fifth graders sat with their desks facing a chalkboard on one of the classroom walls, and the sixth graders sat with their desks facing a chalkboard in another direction in the room. Mrs. Clark would deliver instruction to one grade level, issue an assignment, then head over to the other grade level, deliver instruction, then issue an assignment to those students. I didn't realize how much of a challenge Mrs. Clark's job must have been until I became an educator myself about fifteen years later.

As far as basketball, my game improved when, as a fifth grader, I attended recess with the sixth graders from my class. Often, I was the only fifth grader to play with and against the sixth-grade boys. Some of my fellow fifth-grade classmates would play games other than basketball while others would attempt to play but would not get picked for a team. I was proud of the fact that the bigger, taller, stronger sixth graders respected my game enough to choose me to play. Although I was not the best player on the court when I was going up against them, I was satisfied with contributing and playing my best.

My love for basketball continued to grow through elementary school and into junior high school, where, as a seventh grader, I earned a spot on the seventh- through ninth-grade junior high squad. My twelve-year-old body was significantly more underdeveloped than my teammates' bodies, who were as old as fifteen. I stood about five foot six and weighed just over 100 pounds, while some teammates were taller than six feet and easily outweighed me by fifty pounds or more.

I remember hearing the announcement for basketball tryouts. I was excited *and* nervous. I had never played organized ball before junior high. I had played with my neighborhood friends in my backyard, on the blacktop during elementary school recess, and with family in Tipton County when we visited my grandparents; but I had never played for a team with jerseys, referees, and a game clock. Still, as excited as I was, my mom nearly deflated my hoop dreams before I ever donned a Wildcat jersey.

My mother got baptized as a Jehovah's Witness when I was two years old, and according to her religious beliefs, joining the school team was unacceptable because I would be willfully subjecting myself to bad associates. Momma tried her best to shelter her sons from any sort of temptation that could lead to misconduct or immoral behavior. She knew that many of the boys on the basketball team used profanity and were sexually active. She would often ask the neighborhood boys to leave our backyard for cursing or making inappropriate remarks. Her reputation was so well known in the neighborhood that the most troublesome young men in the community would shush each other and avoid foul language in her presence.

Momma did not want me on that basketball team. In fact, she forbade me to join. She told me no when I asked for permission to stay after school for tryouts, but I didn't obey her. I put my basketball shoes in my backpack along with my hooping shorts, and I stayed after school to try to get on the team.

I hustled my hardest, and I shot my shots. I couldn't just let the chance to play the game I loved so dearly pass me by. I had to go for it no matter what, even if it meant disobeying Momma.

That day, when I arrived home late, Momma was livid, fussing and screaming about what I'd done. For the most part, I was an obedient child. I fully understood that her yes meant yes and her no meant no, and most of the time I listened. But this was the basketball team! *This is my first step to the NBA*, I thought. I might have been an honor roll student who tested intellectually gifted and went to worship three times a week with his mother, but I was also a kid with dreams of playing in the NBA just like millions of kids around the world. Now, as Momma asked me where I had been, I was honest. I wasn't ashamed or afraid, and I didn't feel like I had done anything wrong. I hadn't been out stealing. I hadn't been selling or using drugs. I hadn't been loitering or using profanity around my elders. All I had done was try out for basketball. I was willing to endure whatever punishment Momma would mete out.

After I told Momma where I'd been that afternoon, she broke my heart when she told me I wouldn't be able to join the team even if I made the final cut. And I *did* make the team. I was the only seventh grader selected to play with eighth and ninth graders. I don't remember how long it took Coach Moore to provide the final list, but when I saw my name on the Westside Junior High School Boys' basketball team roster, I shot my fists up in the air and smiled. Momma didn't care one bit though. All she was concerned with was keeping me safe from the wicked influences of the world.

Later, Momma would be diagnosed with paranoid schizophrenia. I truly believe that that mental illness played a serious role in her desire to keep me sheltered. She was in a constant state of distrust during those times and kept her word by trying to prevent me from playing basketball at school. But thank goodness for my father. He interceded on my behalf to allow me to join the team. He saw no problem with me playing. In fact, he was proud of me. I come from a family of athletes, on both of my parents' sides. My older brothers played football, basketball, and ran track in school too.

Meanwhile, Momma made it clear that I would be allowed to play basketball because of my dad only. She said that I "went over" her head and got my father's approval and she had to comply because he was the head of the household. For Momma, this was a catch-22. On the one hand, her religious convictions had influenced her decision to forbid me to join the team. On the other hand, those same convictions caused her to yield to my father's authority as the leader of our home. My main concern as a twelve-year-old was simply being able to play the game I loved for the school I loved. I played my seventh-grade year, and I made the junior high team again in my eighth-grade year—great training. Then, in my ninth-grade year, I was primed and ready to be the primary player, but a change in the educational system put a big dent in my plans.

For years, elementary school in Memphis was from kindergarten through sixth grade; junior high, from seventh through ninth grade; and high school, from tenth through twelfth grade—at least that's the way my schools were set up. My ninth-grade year, the landscape changed. Now, elementary school spanned from kindergarten through fifth grade; junior high, from sixth through eighth grade; and high school, from ninth through twelfth grade. What did all that mean for me? It meant that instead of being the most experienced player on my junior high team as a ninth grader, I was forced, once again, to be the youngest player among a group of bigger, stronger, older, and more experienced players. My only choice as a high school freshman was to earn a spot on our varsity basketball team. My only thirteen-year-old choice was to compete with and against eighteen- and nineteen-year-old students for the opportunity to make that team. I was not happy about this news at all.

I had spent two years playing behind bigger, stronger, and older players—paying my dues and earning my stripes. After two years of working my tail off and waiting my turn, I was ready to be "the man." But then I showed up to school my freshman year to find myself at the back of the pack all over again.

My only choice: Meet the new challenge. The decision to abandon the junior high format and move the ninth grade to the high schools was far beyond my control. I had to rise to the challenge of once again competing with the big boys if I wanted to play basketball at Westside High. With no time to cry about my situation, I worked hard in the offseason and at tryouts to earn a spot on our varsity basketball team.

I was the youngest player on the team. I was the shortest player on the team. I was the thinnest player on the team, but despite all of that, I was on the team.

THE TAKEAWAY

I had worked tirelessly to get what I wanted despite the fact that my parents were at odds throughout the majority of my childhood, even separating at times. Basketball gave me a goal to aspire to and achieve. I did not let my age, physical stature, lack of experience, or any other factor—including my mother's efforts to prevent me from playing—stop me from working toward what I wanted. In fact, the work ethic I developed from pursuing my dream to play basketball helped me become the hard worker I am today. Although developing as a basketball player was ultimately a personal decision, I knew that keeping my grades up and displaying appropriate behavior were required for me to play. Not only did my desire to play basketball fuel my work ethic, it also helped me manage my ACEs.

The moral of this story: Steer traumatized students toward activities that may help them focus and develop a high-quality work ethic. Additionally, if a student displays a passion for a healthy activity, whether it be sports, music, or some other worthy pursuit, but he or she faces parental or other opposition, you may want to intervene to make a case on their behalf about the importance of activity participation. That intervention could be the difference between them stagnating or achieving success.

CHAPTER 2

CHOOSE BATTLES WISELY

Choosing battles wisely is grounded in another cliché. Many clichés we use daily are based in wisdom. If you think about it, they become popular because so many people consider the advice they offer as so helpful that they repeat them over and over. In regard to choosing your battles wisely, remember that you only have twenty-four hours in a day, and you only have so much energy you can exert throughout the course of a day.

I know all of this all too well. You see, I used to battle a lot. I spoke my mind without forethought, and some people considered me a person who would say the first thing that crossed his mind. This stemmed from my home experiences. I remember when my dad had to serve weekend time in jail due to legal infractions related to his drinking. I remember when the police took my mom away in a police car for stabbing my dad. I remember seeing my mom beaten. I remember the pain of losing my brother. So, I was an angry young man at times. I felt like everything that could have gone wrong in my life went wrong, and I didn't care if a teacher or classmate didn't like my choice of words. I am fortunate to have matured past such a foolish way of representing myself. I now understand the importance of considering the words in my head before I allow them to come out of my mouth. It is difficult to learn by listening and watching if you are always talking. It is also difficult to be at peace if you are always fighting.

Even though there will be times when fighting will be the best choice, make sure you are helping your students or children fight for something they believe in, not something that will cause undo hurt. The ways we spend our time and the causes we fight for will define our existences on this earth. The following story from my life shows how and why I avoided a fight that wasn't mine. It can be used as an example for your students or children to help them choose their battles wisely.

SCHOOLWIDE FIGHT

When I was in the eleventh grade, an altercation between two Westside High School students from different neighborhoods escalated into a turf war between students from those different 'hoods.

Some of my basketball teammates were at the core of the incident. The football and basketball teams were close. Many of the basketball players played football too, and most players for both teams were from Frayser, my neighborhood. A similar kinship existed between the students who were bussed to Westside from various parts of North Memphis. Everyone pretty much stuck together.

The incident was not gang related. I mention this because it bothers me when altercations in black neighborhoods are classified as gang related when they are not. Most of the students I associated with in high school were not gang members, although some of them were. Sometimes kids who have grown up together, laughed and cried together, toiled on the practice field and won and lost together, become more than friends. Sometimes they are closer than brothers.

All of this leads me to this memory: My father told me that I should never let my brother see physical harm without helping him. He didn't teach me to start fights or to be a bully, but he taught me to defend myself and my family. We were allowed to fight others one-on-one and not to jump people. When someone else decides not to fight fair, then I was taught to defend myself and my family. I would stand and make sure no one from the outside interfered if one of my brothers was in a one-on-one fistfight. The situation at Westside was much the same.

One of my teammates was at the core of the flare-up. He had a beef with a student who rode the bus. It had already gotten way out of hand by the time I even knew what was going on. There had been a round of fights that morning in the cafeteria before I got to school. I remember being told that my teammate had thrown a chair at a student who was sitting at another table and that an all-out brawl had broken out from there.

Terrance "Gamp" Potts was one of my friends. He was smart and funny, and he liked to rap. We joked around in class and in the halls and had a mutual respect for each other. He rode the bus to school and did not live in my neighborhood.

Our school had an occasional fight from time to time, just like any other school, but Westside was far from a war zone. This time was different though. The tension in my high school was thick. You could feel it in the hallways. The athletes and students from Frayser were hanging together closer, and the students who rode the bus were doing the same.

Gamp and I took several classes together that year, and we both knew what was going on. The rumor in school was that the fight that morning was not the end of the beef and that there would be more fighting at lunch and after school. I don't remember the conversation verbatim, but I do remember what

Gamp said after he approached me: that we were still cool despite the animosity between his neighborhood and mine. He also said he was going to fight with the kids from his neighborhood when it went down and that he expected me to fight with my friends from Frayser.

This was the kicker though: He told me I should go one way and he would go the other way when the two of us were near each other during the fight. He didn't want to go to blows with me. He didn't want to ruin our friendship, which was based on mutual respect and dignity.

I felt that all I could do was agree to the terms. I also felt several emotions. I was proud that he respected me and our friendship enough to think ahead about the possibility of us standing toe to toe in opposition. I was confused about how it had come to the point of a neighborhood versus neighborhood fight. And I was nervous about being in a brawl where I had no idea exactly how many people would be trying to knock me the hell out.

I didn't know I was a diplomat. I didn't know that I could make friends in any environment with people from different backgrounds and circumstances than mine. I just knew that I was cool with a lot of the guys who rode the bus and I was cool with the kids I had grown up with in Frayser and represented Westside with on the basketball team.

Fortunately, there was no fight at lunch or after school. Our school administration and some teachers had stepped in and talked to some of the key players in the morning incident. I think some suspensions were issued and some students went home early that day as well. I learned lessons about myself and about people in general too. I learned that I wasn't a follower. My mind had not instantly gone into fight mode when I found out there had been an incident that morning. Some of the students on both sides of the issue had been ready to fight simply because there was an opportunity to do so. But as for me, I really just wanted to know how the whole thing started.

I also learned that some people are waiting on an excuse to snap. It amazed me to witness the amount of rage many of the students at my school had trapped inside them. I think about the fact that I don't know who is on the verge of going postal or Columbine when I deal with people. I don't appreciate unnecessary violence. Oftentimes, there's a better way to resolve a disagreement.

Moving forward, I became more cautious about who I was loyal to. I knew that my parents would be highly upset to ever hear that I was involved in a fight that had nothing to do with me personally. Years later, I was involved in one fistfight after that incident, and that was because a twenty-four-year-old man took a swing at my sixteen-year-old brother. This happened during a pickup basketball game at a local community center when I was twenty-one. We are all fortunate that the police were not called because we could have all been taken into custody and prosecuted.

Fistfighting is a stupid option. I saw that truth in my role as a middle school dean. Peaceful problem-solving just makes sense. People can usually resolve the conflicts that might lead to fights if they put forth the effort. I teach my students to walk away from potentially hostile situations and be the bigger person by keeping a steady head when conflict arises. Believe it or not, that's the easy part. There are battles that don't involve fists or weapons too.

There will be times when a person has to take a stand and times where they will decide that speaking on a certain subject is not worth the energy. Only that person can determine which battles are worth fighting and which ones are not. My advice is to help your student or child consider the big picture and ask themselves how fighting this particular fight will help them *live* the life they ultimately want. Also, encourage them to ask themselves if avoiding a fight will help them *stay on track to arrive* at the life they ultimately want. They might not make the best choice each time, but at least they may think through all of their options before they decide to fight. Show them that making a move in life is just like making a move in a game of chess—you always make your next move your best move. And if you don't know how to play chess yet, then learn how to play and play often to improve your decision making.

THE TAKEAWAY

How could a trauma-informed approach help students who choose to fight? Keep in mind that the issue igniting the potential fight is probably not what's "really" driving the students' behavior. As Sporleder and Forbes write in *The Trauma-Informed School*, it's likely caused by something outside of school and is "never about the issue at hand" but "goes much deeper." That being said, are we providing these students opportunities to calm down, or are we saying things like, "If you really wanna fight, you should go ahead and do it"? Are we labeling students as fighters and letting them be who we think they are, or are we teaching them how to de-escalate and self-regulate, as Sporleder and Forbes advise? Are we waiting for the student to fight so we can call the police or suspend them, or are we providing all the support we can and disciplining them through the context of the relationship?

When you speak with a student in such a situation, ask them questions like: *Is this your fight? If so, why? What is the outcome that you really want from choosing this battle? If you choose this battle, how can you approach this situation and get the results you want with the least amount of conflict or harm?* Asking these types of questions will allow you to help your students choose battles wisely.

CHAPTER 3

DEVELOP TALENTS

We often enjoy the things we're good at, and we are often good at things we enjoy. In my personal life and in others' lives, I have observed that optimum results occur when we focus on our strengths and our natural talents. To go anywhere worth going in life, you must develop your talents.

While the United States Declaration of Independence states that "all men are created equal," we are created with different skill sets, gifts, talents, and abilities. While many people find fulfillment by using their talents to create and follow their own dreams, many people are miserable because they have not found their purpose. It is the duty of parents, educators, and leaders to help youth develop their talents, and this includes traumatized children. This chapter shows how adults helped me develop my talents as a writer to move my life forward. Their examples can help you in your work with children dealing with ACEs.

TEEN WRITER

Coach Richardson was a short and burly white guy from Chicago. I don't remember if he ever told us how he landed in

Memphis as an English teacher, but he was certainly unlike any teacher I had ever had. Every teacher I'd had in elementary school was female. The librarians and cafeteria workers who served Westside Elementary School were all female too. As a matter of fact, I can only remember three male employees in the entire school—the principal, Mike D. Rowland; a third-grade teacher, Jeffery Akins; and the building engineer, Larry Marshall.

There were a few male teachers when I got to junior high, but the staff was still mostly female. Then in high school, the principal was a black man named William Hudson, and Mr. Nabors, a white man, was the assistant principal. The physical education teacher and football coach was a black man named Richard Horner. The music teacher and two ROTC teachers were brothers as well. The history teacher was a white guy named Frank Fowler and Mike Boldreghini, Italian, was a science teacher and basketball coach.

Richardson arrived at Westside High my ninth-grade year, and I was assigned to his English class. He didn't smile as much as the other teachers. He didn't seem to be as friendly. He drank coffee all day it seemed, and pictures of himself as a boxer stood on his desk. He was interesting to me because he seemed standoffish; I didn't see him laughing and chatting with the other teachers. He stayed to himself. In retrospect, he might not have been standoffish at all. Maybe he just didn't know any of the other teachers since my freshman year was his first year at Westside. Most of the other teachers were already at the school before that. At any rate, William Richardson fascinated me. He assisted Coach Horner with the football team, and he would later start a wrestling team from the ground up at Westside. Several Westside wrestlers would compete in state championship tournaments under Richardson's tutelage.

One day, Richardson called me to his desk to discuss a writing assignment I had turned in. He told me that I was "a pretty good writer." His recognition and compliment flattered me. Writing was a secret passion of mine. I had been writing poetry since elementary school, but not many people knew it— especially any adults. Richardson might have been the first adult to ever compliment my writing, and I appreciated him for it. Actually, I appreciated the compliment so much that I brought some of my poetry to school for him to read.

During my teenage years, pain packed my poetry. These years were tough in the Matthews household. My father was battling depression and alcoholism, while Momma and my older brother Marland were battling schizophrenia. I was battling with the pressures of meeting the Jehovah's Witness standard, which meant not having friends who were not the children of Jehovah's Witnesses, not celebrating worldly holidays, being forced to preach from door to door in the neighborhood where I went to school, and not participating in extracurricular activities. There were some things about life that I didn't understand and other things that I simply hated.

I didn't understand why my parents argued so much. I didn't understand why my father wouldn't come home some nights. I didn't understand why my mother didn't want me to select my own friends. I didn't understand why she thought the color red was evil or the house was bugged. I didn't understand why she tore up our family pictures or cut up our clothes. Those were things I simply didn't understand. The list of things I hated was much deeper. I hated not being able to hug my mother because she thought there was a "scheme" to accuse her of having sex with her children. I hated not being able to spend time with my father. I hated watching Marland's mind deteriorate from his mental illness. In all honesty, I felt like we lost Marland years before he was found murdered. I hated being confined to my room while my schoolmates played outside, and when I was finally allowed outside, I hated not being able to leave the street and go elsewhere. I got teased about that a lot. "Y'all know Marcus can't go nowhere," the neighborhood kids would say. I really hated that.

Poetry became my outlet. It became my therapy. My passion. My friend. I spent countless nights in my bedroom with pen in hand. To this day, I have hundreds of poems I wrote as a child that no one has ever read.

Richardson earned a place in my secret corridor when he complimented my writing. He was genuine and sincere, even with a permanent frown and coffee on his breath. My poetry surprised him. He didn't know I was dealing with so much pain and that my life was in such turmoil. He started checking on me after that, asking if I was okay. I let him know that I was fine, even though my circumstances were not. Somehow, I internalized all my anger, pain, and disappointment and released it through writing. Writing made me okay.

Richardson continued to read my poetry for the remainder of the schoolyear, and we continued to discuss my state of mind. As freshman year came to an end, he surprised me by engaging my soon-to-be sophomore English teacher, Ms. Poor, in a conversation about my writing. He told her that I was a talented writer and that she should read my poetry as often as possible when she became my teacher. Ms. Poor picked up the torch, as requested, and became my new writing mentor the next school year. I brought her poetry to read, just as I had with Richardson, and we developed a much needed, healthy student-teacher relationship.

I had no idea how badly I really needed mentors and role models. With my mother sick, my dad struggling, and though things were looking from good to great from the outside looking in, I was lost. I was lost because everything really *was* great at first. We'd had the storybook life: My dad was a handsome fireman; my mom was a beautiful churchgoing housewife; my older brothers were respectful, smart, and athletic; my younger brother was cute as a button, and I was just happy. My sheltered, naïve life had no idea what was in store for it. It were as if the sky had just come crashing down, and while the sky was falling, someone had snatched the land off the earth and dumped all the water in the seas, oceans, lakes, ponds, and rivers over me all at once. I was ducking, hiding, shaking, shivering, falling down, getting up, and standing tall all at the same time. I found my solace in my writing, in basketball, and in those people who supported either one of the two.

Throughout my sophomore year, Ms. Poor served as my teacher and advisor. Fortunately, she was my junior English teacher as well. Westside was such a small high school that teachers often taught more than one grade. Before my senior year, Ms. Poor set me up for the following teacher just as Richardson had done two years prior. She introduced me to Betty Russell, the senior English teacher, and she told Mrs. Russell to be sure to read my poetry when I became her student. By this time, I had become more open to the notion that I was a writer and I had developed a reputation schoolwide, writing poetry for school programs and special occasions.

With that knowledge in mind, Mrs. Russell approached me about applying to be a part of Memphis' first citywide high school newspaper, called *Teen Appeal*. The paper and an accompanying journalism program had resulted from a partnership between the Scripps Howard Foundation, *The Commercial Appeal* newspaper, the University of Memphis, and the Memphis City Schools. Dr. Elinor Grusin, a journalism professor at the University of Memphis, had created it. The program was developed as an outreach effort focused on producing minority journalists from the area. The idea: Recruit potential journalists from Memphis high schools; train them in the fundamental skills of newspaper journalism; mentor them in producing a citywide high school newspaper; provide academic scholarships to pay top performers to major in journalism in college; offer continued support and training through internships at Scripps Howard newspapers; and ultimately produce and hire competent journalists of color to help diversify newsrooms around the country. What a brilliant concept!

Of course, as a high school junior in Frayser, I had no idea of the magnitude of the undertaking I was being introduced to. The program was a big deal, and Mrs. Russell wanted me to take advantage of the opportunity to develop my talent and earn an academic scholarship. She handed me the program application and urged me to fill it out . . . and just like millions of other typical, absentminded high schoolers around the world, I shrugged off her suggestion and did not complete the application. Days, or maybe weeks later, Mrs. Russell saw me in the hallway. Remember, I was not her student at this time. She taught seniors, and I was still a junior. Still, she pulled me to the side and asked me about the application. When I told her I hadn't filled it out, she made me sit down in her classroom right then and there and complete it. Without an argument, I did what I was told.

The program sounded like a good idea. The opportunity to meet students from around the city, write stories, and take pictures sounded good; but filling out an application to do so just wasn't a priority in my life at that time. I was seventeen and more concerned about basketball, dating, and buying clothes and speakers than filling out an application to join an outreach program for prospective journalists. But ultimately, having completed the application due to Mrs. Russell's intervention, I was accepted into the program.

I have not seen Betty Russell since high school. She didn't return to Westside for my senior year. She retired and was replaced by Sandra Edscorn, a first-year teacher. More than twenty years after she taught at Westside, I don't know where Mrs. Russell landed, but I want to thank her. I would give her a great big hug and say, "Thank you for making me sit down and fill out that application that changed my life for the better."

For reading my poetry and encouraging me to persevere, Ms. Poor deserves a big ol' hug too. Richardson and I are connected through social media, and he still teaches and coaches in Memphis. He is also an author himself now. Different teachers helped me in different ways throughout my thirteen years at Westside from elementary to high school graduation, but those three teachers brought me out of my shell as a writer and encouraged me to share my gift with the world. For that, I am eternally grateful.

So, as a participant in the new newspaper program, the first Lionel Linder Journalism Camp at the University of Memphis, I and high school students from various Memphis City Schools spent a week learning how to interview, write, and photograph for newspapers. The first day I stepped on campus, I was blown away. The auditorium was filled with students ready to learn. It was a different atmosphere than what I saw at Westside. Although Westside had dedicated teachers who wanted the best for, and tried to teach, their students, the prevailing school culture and climate there was ultimately not conducive to learning.

At Westside, the air conditioning didn't work, so on really hot days, we would only attend school until ten thirty a.m. Many classes only had enough books for a class set, so we couldn't take books home to do homework. Some teachers never assigned homework. Some teachers never read the assignments they issued us. Sometimes I would purposely write down wrong answers or enter jokes or sarcastic comments on assignments just to see if the teacher would notice. Unfortunately, many times they never did. The fact that I knew that some of my teachers didn't take my work seriously encouraged me to take my school performance less seriously as well. I mean, why find the correct answer if the teacher was going to give me credit for the wrong answer anyway?

Journalism camp was different though. Every adult there seemed to be serious about what was happening. Many of the students seemed serious too. On the first day, I arrived early and observed as much as I could during the continental breakfast that was provided. From there, I walked into the auditorium and sat among students who were all ready to listen and learn. Surprisingly, I liked it. I liked the idea of being surrounded by people who were comfortable doing academic work unlike the prevailing student attitude at Westside that we were there to play around, call each other names, and skip class. The University of Memphis provided me with a new lens to use to look at education and learning.

At the camp, professionals from *The Commercial Appeal* and faculty from the University of Memphis journalism department instructed us. I remember listening to Angus McEachran, the former editor-in-chief of *The Commercial Appeal*, and Otis Sanford, who was then deputy managing editor, and meeting Judith Clabes, former CEO of the Scripps Howard Foundation. Tara Miligan was the project coordinator, and Aimee Edmonson was her assistant. They were my first writing coaches. Mostly, I remember Dr. Elinor Kelley Grusin, my other mother. She loved my seventeen-year-old enthusiasm. I hadn't ever been surrounded by that many working professionals in my life.

At the end of one of our lunch breaks at the camp, I stood behind the podium in the Meeman Journalism Building and spouted a Forrest Gump impression into the microphone. The students and the professionals started peeping into the auditorium to see who the clown was who had the audacity to jump on the mic. Dr. Grusin loved my impression and said I should have been doing it from the start of the camp to wake everybody up. She's been looking out for me ever since. I completed the camp, learned a lot that week, and set my sites on becoming a professional journalist.

The story I deem most memorable during my tenure as a staffer at *Teen Appeal*, the newspaper that resulted from the camp and that I wrote for during the regular school year, was about Westside Elementary being renovated, which necessitated that some of its fifth and sixth graders attend classes in my high school. I simply asked a few of the elementary children who were in our high school building how they felt. One child responded, "Scared."

I followed up by asking that child what scared him, and he said, "I'm scared of dying." I led the story with that exact quote. The college students who were on staff at the University of Memphis newspaper, *The Daily Helmsman*, commented on how good that quote was. My new principal at Westside High, Victor Carr, even found a new respect for my position as the mouthpiece and reporter for my school.

Writing for *Teen Appeal* was one of the most influential experiences in my life. It made me a better writer through the on-the-job training. It introduced me to new people who would help me make crucial life decisions, apply for scholarships and financial aid, and land internships and jobs. I even coined the newspaper's slogan, "Giving Truth to Memphis Youth." The *Teen Appeal* displayed that slogan on its banner for years until the day that it ceased production.

After a year as a *Teen Appeal* staffer, I received the first annual *Teen Appeal* scholarship. At that time, only two of those scholarships were awarded. I accepted the award and attended the University of Memphis to major in journalism. My parents could not provide financial support, so my instructors Tara Miligan and Aimee Edmonson offered strong references to the school's scholarship office so that I might receive additional financial aid.

While attending Memphis, I completed successful internships with the Associated Press, *The Commercial Appeal*, the *Birmingham Post-Herald*, and the Memphis Grizzlies (NBA) as an undergraduate journalism major. I also received the University of Memphis Journalism Department Newspaper/Editorial Student of the Year Award and the National Association of Black Journalists University of Memphis Chapter's Excellence Award in Sports Writing.

THE TAKEAWAY

Due to the encouragement and nurturing of teachers, I developed my talent as a storyteller and writer and went on to attend a journalism camp that would change the trajectory of my future. Participating in the camp enabled me to receive an academic scholarship to the University of Memphis and earn a bachelor's degree in journalism. I gained immeasurable experience, opportunities, and relationships during my undergraduate years. I also gained the foundation required to pursue the graduate degree that would lead me to a career as an educator and to earn a doctorate in education. I was a child who suffered from multiple severe adverse childhood experiences. The teachers who were patient and considerate—those who took a personal interest in me—helped me overcome my ACEs.

Helping students identify and develop their talents will open doors for them and lead them to success. When you see what they shine in, help them appreciate their talent and give them the tools and information to take it to the next level.

CHAPTER 4

KEEP YOUR BEST FOOT FORWARD

Please read the following story and understand that the world is watching your student. Some see children suffering from ACEs as circus clowns when they are struggling, while others see them as symbols of hope when they thrive. Very few people will understand them, but everyone in the world is watching.

Onlookers want to see what the child is made of—who they really are: Do they meet all the stereotypes? Will they make it? Will they crack? When will they finally lose it? Years ago, I reached a point where I realized that the way I carried myself really mattered. This is a concept that is very important to communicate to your students or children. The following story shows why.

CRUISIN'

Beale Street in Memphis is one of the most famous streets in the world. The street, which runs nearly two miles from the Mississippi River into downtown, serves as a tourist attraction known for mouthwatering barbecue and live blues music. Tourists and locals also enjoy taking horse-drawn carriage rides, walking the Beale Street strip, watching the famous Beale Street Flippers, and more.

"Flicking" was a form of entertainment that many young people enjoyed on and around Beale Street when I was a teenager and in my early twenties. The police later named the activity "cruising" and made it illegal. Young people, and some older people, would clean their cars, shine their wheels and tires, and ride up and down the street. A 2006 article in *The Commercial Appeal* highlighted how cruising was still a problem in downtown. One of the people interviewed said that traffic would often be backed up due to cruising.

My friends and I used to cruise, and we didn't care how tourists, pedestrians, or anyone else felt about it. It was inexpensive entertainment. You could see young black guys hanging out of their car windows and sunroofs as they slowly paraded up and down the downtown streets. We played our music loud and shouted out the names of the neighborhoods from which we came. We were immature, rebellious children having a good time at the expense of public order and tranquility, and I was totally cool with that until the summer I landed my first internship—yet another opportunity to develop my talents and get more exposure to the professional world.

You couldn't tell me I wasn't the man my first day at *The Commercial Appeal*. I had an afro like Ice Cube in the movie *Higher Learning* and a swagger like LL Cool J in his "I'm Bad" video. Still, after an hour at the *Appeal*, I was floored. That Monday morning, I walked into the office of Gary Robinson, assistant sports editor and my direct supervisor, and he explained how things would work. I would cover sports stories due by that night's deadline three days of the week; the other two days, I would work with the copy desk to proof stories, headlines, and cutlines for mistakes and accuracy.

Gary showed me to my computer station, set up my email and

voicemail, and then left me alone for about an hour to familiarize myself with the software. I was in awe, asking myself, *Is this how corporate America works?* My work at *The Daily Helmsman* had prepared me skillwise, but I had never experienced an office environment. I was expecting a busy room full of buzzing reporters and editors smoking cigars and screaming, "Write, write, write!"

The sports department was on a floor away from the metro desk and all other writers. Plus, I reported to work around ten a.m., the time that sports writers aren't working unless they're covering golf or a morning press conference. Things were quiet and arranged. My new job was a far cry from stocking bleach or stacking detergent at Fred's.

It also wasn't chasing busy shoppers through the Raleigh Springs Mall, rotating watermelons at Piggly Wiggly, or pushing and pulling freight and loading planes at FedEx, all jobs I'd had. This was on another level. I was a small cog in a large wheel. I would be writing stories all of Memphis would read. Though I lived in a poor apartment in a poor neighborhood, I had come a long way.

The exposure to corporate America I gained that summer opened my eyes to the need to stop acting a fool in public. There wasn't going to be any more riding down Beale Street yelling "Noooorth Memphis" at the top of my lungs. No more hanging out the back of Charmin's Jeep at Denim and Diamonds, a local club, riding girls around like his vehicle was a Ferris wheel. No more getting hammered drunk downtown and saying the first thing that came to my mind to the first person who let me say it. As a sports writer, I felt like a celebrity. I didn't want to be seen acting a fool on the town one night and have the same person see me covering their child's basketball game for the local paper the next night. I also started to feel I would have a professional future and all the writing and waking up at five a.m. to catch the bus to college might actually pay off.

The internship went well. I wrote a lot and learned even more. I even made the paper's front page a few times. What I consider more important than those things though is that I gained more exposure. I was exposed to people with different backgrounds and values than mine and to a new definition of what it meant to go to work. I also began to believe I could impact lives with the gift I was given by God Himself.

THE TAKEAWAY

Our students should understand that the image they present to the world matters. Although they might think they know who they are, most of the people who will be looking at them every day will not. American society, primarily through pop culture and the media, has painted a negative picture of what it means to come from an adverse situation. Instead of focusing on our intellect, resiliency, loyalty, and natural abilities, we are often perpetuated as welfare cases in need of pity.

Cruising Beale Street didn't make me an evil person. However, my life could have taken a turn for the worse if one of my editors or colleagues at the *Appeal* had seen me cruising Beale, screaming out of a car window, and holding up traffic while he was trying to take his wife and kids out for dinner at a nice downtown restaurant. I could have been denied opportunities simply because I gave the impression that I was not a law-abiding citizen. With the popularity of social media, be mindful of what your students post on the internet. Encourage them to think about their poses in their pictures, signs they might make with their hands, what they wear, what people, items, and images they are pictured with, and the comments they post or even repost from another account. Help them understand that the image they project to the world can expand or limit their opportunities. In other words, as Sporleder and Forbes say in *The Trauma-Informed School*, help them self-regulate. As you help the children in your life regulate their own self-image and keep their best foot forward, you are providing a trauma-informed approach in your mentorship.

CHAPTER 5

FIND GOOD FRIENDS

Every day that I can remember as a child, Momma quoted Scriptures. Many of them were recycled because she had her favorites that she liked to recite over and over. Among those she commonly cited was 1 Corinthians 15:33: "Bad associations spoil useful habits."

She would quote that Scripture in reference to the friends I chose. I used to think that Momma just didn't want me to have any fun back then, but now I realize that she simply wanted the best for me, and she knew that the people I spent the most time with would have a tremendous effect on my life, which they did. The following chapter focuses on key friends over the course of my life and how they impacted me. As you read it, consider who the children in your life befriend and whether or how you should encourage those friendships.

DISCO

Disco was my best friend through much of junior high and high school. He was, and still is, one of the smartest and most creative and artistic people I know. He became my barber when

I was about twelve. It actually hurt my dad's feelings when Disco started doing my hair because Pop had pretty much been my barber up to that point. Disco was about fourteen when I became his "client." Dad said Disco did a good job.

Disco could draw too. He later learned to tattoo. He could also fix stuff. He was a philosopher of sorts as well. When we got older, we would talk about life choices, and he would often say, "There are advantages and disadvantages to every situation." I think about those words quite often now that he is locked away in prison.

My mom was strict about where I went and who I hung around, so I did not have many friends. Momma loved my childhood partner Disco though. She still does.

She was sad when she heard he was arrested—again. He was charged with using a gun to commit a felony and evading arrest, according to a crime report in *The Commercial Appeal*.

Now, I have finished my third college degree, a doctorate, and he is serving time for his third conviction, a felony. It boggles my mind to think that two people from seemingly the same circumstances with similar personalities and interests can end up worlds apart.

Quite often, I hear that I'm ahead of the game because I got my education out of the way at an early age. A couple of advantages are that my credentials look good on a resume and I shouldn't have to worry about finishing up my schooling when I have a wife and children to support. One disadvantage is that I spent much of my youth cooped up in a classroom, library, or computer lab instead of enjoying the beautiful gifts present in the world around me. Another disadvantage is that I might not have children or might be too old to run and play with them if I don't get a move on it!

This reminds me that Disco always wanted me to look at both sides of an issue before I made a decision. He kept me grounded although he walked around with his head all up in the clouds.

He always wanted to protect me once our lives began going in separate directions. For instance, some years ago, he wanted to personally investigate who burglarized my house. From there he wanted to be judge, jury, and executioner as well. I chose to simply file a police report and improve my home security.

**

Disco made a couple of stops in jail while I was going to school. He befriended criminals, and I befriended academics. He became more street, and I became more mainstream. We both became more institutionalized.

We had a few friends in common from the old days, but we had both been introduced to new worlds by the time we were adults. Disco put me on a pedestal when I visited him and his other friends were around. He would brag about my academic accomplishments as if he had accomplished them himself. I would be proud and uncomfortable at the same time. I told him often, and I meant it, that he was smart enough to do the things I had done academically. He might have had the potential to do more.

People tell me that I'm smart, and I know I have the capability to grasp concepts quicker than some others, but I know there are sharper tacks in the box than me too. There is much more that I don't know than there is that I do know. I also believe that a wise man can learn from a fool, although a fool won't learn from a wise man. I try to act like a wise man although I act as a foolish man from time to time. That's where I think Disco and I are different. He wouldn't listen to a person unless he feels like they are just as smart or smarter than him. And that is a short list of people. My brother from another mother wanted to outsmart the system instead of learning to work from within it.

I know he feels me. I hope no one reading this passage gets the impression that I'm throwing my old friend under the bus. I love that man. His children call me "Uncle." I check up on his wife from time to time to see if the family is okay and to see how Disco is holding up while he's locked up. I sincerely believe I speak on behalf of every person who loves Disco when I say I wish he would have slowed down just enough to get a plan together and execute it.

Disco's wife interrupted a conversation between Disco and me one day to say she wished he would take some of the advice he was giving me. She would hear bits and pieces of our conversations during my separation and divorce—yes, I was once married. Disco wanted me to be fair to my ex-wife and to myself. I would sit there in his kitchen and run down scenarios to him as we played chess and drank Hennessey: *If she and I get back together, then . . . If we remain apart, then . . .* When I mentioned a positive point, Disco would reply, "Okay. Now what's the disadvantage?" When I mentioned a negative point, he would reply, "Okay. But what's the advantage?"

He never once told me to reconcile with my ex-wife, nor did he ever tell me not to stay with her. Friends don't tell friends how to live their lives. Friends support friends the best way they can, which is usually by listening, offering sound advice when it's asked for, and supporting the decisions they make. That's what made Disco such a good friend. He listened, he gave great advice, and he supported me.

Disco never asked my opinion about drug use. I don't know the degree to which he ever talked to anyone about the subject. It wasn't a big deal to see a person who was high on cocaine where we grew up either. I understood that many snort powder just as casually as other people have a drink of wine or smoke a cigarette or a blunt. Being high on cocaine was just too much for me from what I saw though. I never wanted to be revved up that high. That's my preference, however. It was never my place to tell another person what to put inside their body.

Once, I told Disco about a TV special I had watched about cocaine. I told him I never knew the drug was produced by extracting the active ingredient from the plant it comes from and combining that with more extractions from other plants to make it powerful. It amazed me that cocaine was power multiplied by power. Some scientist created the drug by accident. I thought that was unnatural because the part of the plant that isn't used for cocaine is simply thrown away.

Disco went on to tell me more about cocaine than I had learned from the television show. His point was not to show me up. It was to let me know that he knew exactly what he was doing, period.

I wish we had talked more about cocaine though. I wish he had come to me to discuss a desire to quit. I would have told him I'm glad he trusted me enough to talk to me. I would have told him his family and all his real friends would be happy about his decision. I would have told him that it was more likely he would be around to spend time with his sons and his daughter if he had stuck to his decision. I would have told him he was more likely to stay focused enough to finish barber school and become a licensed barber without drugs. But I didn't say it. I never said, "You need to stop." I never asked him to quit. And now that he is in prison—again—I have to ask myself, *What kind of friend am I?*

That makes me think about the kind of friend Disco has been to me. As a youth, I would visit with him at his mother's beauty salon, or he would come over to my place and hang out with me at least a couple of times a week. I remember when an ex-girlfriend cheated on me, and I rushed to the salon to tell him about it. I was about fifteen.

The girl went to Wooddale, on the other side of the city from my school. A mutual friend had shown me a picture of her one day, and I had asked my friend to give her my phone number. After a few phone conversations, never having seen each other in person, we were boyfriend and girlfriend—true puppy love. Soon afterward, she spent a night with our mutual friend one weekend and I rode my bike more than ten miles to see her. We did a bunch of kissing, and that was that.

I was in the kitchen shaping up some ground beef for a hamburger one day, and my fries were baking in the oven. The phone rang. I picked up the receiver only to have my teenage heart broken into pieces. "I can't be your girlfriend no more," she said. I remember that verbatim!

"Why?" I asked. "What's wrong?"

She was a freshman. She said that she and an upperclassman had had been together at school that day.

I left my ground beef on the kitchen counter, hung up the phone, and started running. I ran from my house up to Disco's momma's shop.

I had been growing a 'fro for a few months. I used to grow my hair at random back in the day. I got to the shop and told Disco everything that happened. After that, I sat in the barber chair and told him to cut my 'fro off. He hesitated and asked me if I was sure, then he set about cutting my hair. It was my way of cutting my old girlfriend off. Disco was there for me.

I will never forget all the free haircuts Disco gave me when we were growing up, although our lives went in separate directions and we didn't hang out as much throughout high school and much of our early twenties. I remember times when Pop's gambling ate up our allowances and left Greg, my younger brother, and me without money to pay for a haircut. Disco would make sure my little brother and I looked sharp and didn't miss a beat. He would buy me food on the days I hung out with him at his mom's shop too. He was one of the most genuine people I had ever met, and he still is to this day.

Disco and I started seeing each other again more than a decade ago. He was back with his wife and son after serving a jail sentence. We were older, more mature, both married, and attempting to be calmer, more conservative guys. I was a schoolteacher and Disco said he would finish earning his barber license and soon thereafter go into business for himself. We mostly played chess and talked about life over Hennessey. Eventually, he was sidetracked away from his goal of barbering and I was sidetracked from living happily ever after with the woman who would become my ex-wife.

Disco has a family that loves him, and I hope he doesn't lose them because they can't stand to deal with his foolishness and feel they are better off without him. Trust me, it happens. I look forward to seeing my friend as a free and changed man. Much of the difference in our lives centers around the associates we chose. My good friend chose to surround himself with gang members and criminals, while I chose to surround myself with students and professionals. Hopefully, my good friend will choose his associates more wisely once he has served his debt to society.

B-DUBB

In high school, I was always the shortest person on the basketball team. I wasn't physically overpowering, and though I generally played well, I couldn't dunk the basketball. I think it's safe to say no one on the team worked harder than me. One of my favorite quotes is from a song where rapper T.I. says, "Every single thing I ever did was done heavily." His statement applies to me as well.

I asked my junior high coach, Paulette Moore, what I could do to get better. She told me to shoot every day. She said not to let the ball bounce three times before I had picked it up to shoot again. And that's exactly what I did. I took shots until my coaches said it was time for me to go. When I got home, I would shoot in my backyard.

Blake Christopher Williams, aka "B-Dubb," was our starting point guard, and I backed him up. B-Dubb was a year older than me and about five or six inches taller. He was an outstanding basketball player too. I don't know if he knew it or not, but he motivated the hell out of me. B-Dubb had been playing organized basketball via the Amateur Athletic Union (AAU) circuit for years before we became teammates in junior high. My training up to that point had been playing with kids at recess back in elementary school, with kids from the neighborhood in my backyard, and with my older brothers on an occasional trip to the park.

B-Dubb was smooth and composed on the court. I suppose years of playing in front of crowds had numbed much of the nervousness. The first time Coach Moore put me in the game, I was scared stiff. We were playing White Station, and I got my pocket picked. The defender slapped the ball right out of my hand and went the other way for a layup. I can still hear Coach Moore say, "He ain't ready! Go get him outta there." I was pulled from the game at the next dead ball. Later, I returned and made a free throw that put my team up by one point with seconds left to play and we went on to beat White Station by one point.

To simulate shooting over outstretched arms, in my backyard I used to shoot over a broomstick that I had situated on top of a couple of buckets. I have B-Dubb to thank for that too. It took a lot of work to get a good shot against that guy. His arms were longer than mine in addition to the five- or six-inch height advantage he boasted. I could shoot though. I wasn't going to give up because everyone else was taller than me. It was a matter of figuring out what I could do to create my own advantage and putting in the work to make it a reality.

I enjoyed running in addition to hooping, and I figured out I would have an advantage of my own if I were in better shape than the other players on the court. So, I ran. I used to jog around the neighborhood, going for miles at a time. I might have had the best wind on the squad from ninth grade onward. I even joined the cross country team in eleventh grade and competed in two state championships as a co-captain. I cared more about basketball though. I had figured out I would have to be a worrisome, pesky dog if I wanted to be a contributing factor on my team.

I played relentless defense. I tried my best to get under the skin of opposing guards. I would defend them the length of the floor and stay as close as I could to them, whether or not they had the basketball. There is nothing more aggravating to an offensive player than a defender who will not let them breathe. My goal was to get my opponent so frustrated by my presence that he didn't even want the ball, and it worked!

B-Dubb made me a better basketball player. He didn't do it by giving me pointers he learned in AAU, although I learned some tricks from him over the years. B-Dubb made me better by challenging me every day I walked into the gym to practice against him. We were both competitive guys who loved basketball, and we still are to this day. To my knowledge, he and I are the only guys from our high school team who still play regularly. I used to wish I was taller and get upset when people called me short, but I got over it. You can't teach a person how to be six foot nine, but you can teach someone how to defend a six-foot-nine player. You can't teach fast, but you can teach a defender how to use an opponent's speed to the defender's advantage.

I learned how to look for my advantage in a situation by playing against players who had obvious advantages. I learned to use my brain when my body alone wasn't enough. I'm glad I learned to think, because my brain has taken me a long way in life. I learned to apply my brain and work ethic to whatever task faced me, and one of my first challenges was battling an older, taller, more polished basketball player who became a friend for life.

I learned to surround myself with people who challenge me to be my best in part because of my relationship with B-Dubb and other athletes like my cross country teammates Terrance White, Andrew Rodgers, Corey Massey, and Daniel Coleman.

All those guys were outperforming me when I joined the cross country team my junior year, but I was our top runner by the time that year ended. Daniel and I were named co-captains the following year.

Rarecus Williamson, Andrew Rodgers, Jason Jones, and Antuan Knapp were other guards on our basketball team along with B-Dubb and me, and I was the youngest of the bunch. We all competed for minutes on the court at the same position. We were all friends, but we all pushed each other because we all wanted to play. Those guys taught me to keep pushing and never quit despite the odds.

DIDDY

Terrance Clements and I did not get along in junior high or high school. We nearly fought on several occasions. But while our personalities clashed as children, we became close friends as adults.

Westside was such a small school that we didn't have specialist athletes like many of the larger schools. I was a three-sport athlete: basketball, track, and cross country. Terrance (before he was "Diddy") was a four-sport athlete. He played basketball, ran track and cross country with me, and was on the football team.

Competition often breeds success. Magic Johnson and Larry Bird were both successful professional basketball players. They competed against each other year after year and became better athletes because of the constant competition and practice it took each of them to be better the next time they met. Magic's Lakers and Bird's Celtics were rivals. Rivalries can get ugly though. The competition between Terrance and me turned into a rivalry, and our rivalry got ugly too.

Terrance was blunt. I was subtle. He was more of a natural

athlete. I was a student of sport. Many of our differences stemmed from those polarities. We were both arrogant but in totally different ways. We were both smart alecks toward each other. We both knew it, and we both acted the way we did on purpose. We weren't mature enough to appreciate that we both brought a special skill set to our teams. We brought different personalities too. We began to complement each other as adults though.

A couple of mutual friends and former teammates had sons who were playing little league sports sometime around summer 2006. Terrance and I showed up in support, and soon thereafter B-Dubb, the former captain of our basketball team, came up with the idea that we should enter an adult basketball league. We got as many of the fellas as we could find and did just that. We won the Bartlett City League Championship in 2007 and placed second in 2008.

Most of the guys were married or in committed relationships when we started seeing more of each other back in '06. Terrance was the only guy who was truly single. My marriage was on the rocks. By then, my soon-to-be ex-wife had her own apartment. Terrance was one of the closest people to me during the time I was dealing with losing her.

We talked a lot about life and decisions. We made amends in regards to the hostility we had harbored against each other as adolescents. Actually, I found out I had harbored more of a grudge than he had. Much of our childish foolishness was just childish foolishness from his perspective, but it had felt like more to me.

Growing up, I had always remembered a lot of little things many others forgot. I attribute holding certain memories to probably having mulled over scenarios after everyone else had moved on to new business. On several occasions, I might have mentioned things someone did or said years ago that they might not remember. I love telling stories, and you have to remember a story in order to tell it.

I remember the good and the bad, and I will talk about whichever is relevant. Terrance didn't really have anything to get off his chest when it came to me. Or he didn't say anything if he did. Nonetheless, I appreciated being friends with someone who I had known and been associated with throughout most of my adolescence.

Because Terrance would often pick up the tab when we would go hang out, I nicknamed him "Diddy." If there were other guys with us or even if we met a couple of women where we were, Terrance would regularly pay for everyone's food and drinks. I compared him to Bad Boy Records CEO P. Diddy, because P. Diddy had a reputation for spending money without a care.

Diddy and I would throw barbecues in the summer. We would cook and watch sports at my crib one weekend and his crib the next. Although I take credit for teaching the guy how to cook, the thing he gave me credit for has left me shocked and humbled. We were headed out for drinks one night, and he told me he was going back to school to finish his bachelor's degree. Diddy had attended Austin Peay State University after Westside. He had transferred back home after about a year and ended up getting a nice paying job and discontinuing his coursework. He told me, however, that I had motivated him to go back to school after being away from the college environment for nearly a decade. I didn't know what to say to him then, and I really still don't know what to say.

In recent times, I was a groomsman in Diddy's wedding. In our high school days, if you had told either of us that would be the case, we both would have called you crazy. My friendship with Diddy helped me appreciate the importance of appreciating differences and letting bygones be bygones.

We are all navigating life the best way we know how. We are all from different places and are headed in different directions. We all have different life courses. That course changes sometimes, even when we think we know exactly where we're headed. There isn't enough time to live in the past, handle our business for today, and plan for tomorrow. We must be decisive and understand where we are trying to go and what we need to do to get there. My friendship with Diddy helped me see those things as well.

RONNIE

Ronnie was a brother to me when I needed a brother. He didn't have to open up his home to me, but he did. I don't think either of us expected our friendship to flourish the way it did. We spent a lot of time together because we not only lived together, but we worked together at Piggly Wiggly in the daytime and at FedEx at night. We were practically joined at the hip.

People used to say that Ronnie and I spoke a language that no one really understood but the two of us. Our language developed from taking words or phrases from events that took place at the crib or at work. We just plain made up some of the other words and phrases we used. We didn't purposely talk in a way others couldn't understand. We had simply spent so much time together that we had developed our own jargon. It was no different than slang, a language developed when people with commonalities communicate with each other.

Ronnie and I created the word "Preciatory." Something that should be appreciated, like a pretty woman or a sale on Air Force Ones, is preciatory—"preshe" for short. If Ronnie were to tell me he met a nice, attractive girl at the grocery store, I might respond by saying, "Preciatory."

"Bubble" was a multipurpose word back in the day. We used it as a noun to represent something good. If I told Ronnie I made an A on a quiz, he might respond, "That's a bubble."

"Bubblin'" was an adjective as well. It meant to be hype or revved up. A party that had good food and music was bubblin'. It was also a verb. I'm about to bubble means "I'm about to leave." We had a million of 'em. Outsiders would often feel left out of the conversation when Ronnie and I talked to each other.

One time, Ronnie and I went to my oldest brother Terry's house to visit. Terry got frustrated trying to understand what Ronnie and I were saying, so he told us to "stop talkin' that stuff." We just apologized and started laughing because that wasn't the first time that had happened.

When Ronnie and I lived together, he told me that his mother suffered from schizophrenia. When we became friends and my dad was MIA on a bad drug binge, Ronnie's relationship with his father was nearly nonexistent. Throughout our young adulthood, we were each other's anchor. I don't even want to know what might have become of either of us had we not been there for each other during such turbulent times.

After living together for four years, Ronnie and I decided not to continue as roommates. He wanted to leave Memphis, and I planned to move to Covington to live with Madea, my paternal grandmother, who had recently turned eighty. She was alone because the two grandchildren she had raised were headed to college. After Ronnie and I parted ways, we never saw much of each other from that point on. Still, I had grown up, learned how to be responsible, and shared some of the wildest times of my life with that guy.

SMOOTH

When Marcus "Smooth" Moody played basketball for the University of Memphis, I was the *Helmsman's* sports editor and covered the team. Later, he played some pro ball overseas and did a stint of coaching at his alma mater, Overton High School, where I got my first teaching assignment once I started working on my master's degree.

Smooth is popular, knows a lot of people, and knows how to network. I never knew until we became friends how well-suited he is for his nickname. He's a likeable, down-to-earth guy, which is not the way I would describe many of the star athletes I have come across, whether during or following their athletic careers.

I was especially impressed to see him earn his bachelor's degree. I knew he was smart enough, but so many athletes never go back and finish their degrees after their eligibility is up and the ball has stopped bouncing. The degree Smooth earned is a tribute to his strength. Most ballers want to play in the NBA. Though Jay-Z said he's "seen hoop dreams deflate like a true fiend's weight," Smooth was not deterred by not making it to the league.

When Smooth and I saw each other at Overton, we greeted each other with mutual respect. By me being a baller in high school and an avid hoops fan, I appreciated what Smooth had accomplished in his four-year career as a Tiger. He had read my work as sports editor of our college paper and respected my talent as well.

We both ate lunch at the same time at Overton. So, with basketball, college, and age in common, we conversed often and developed a surface friendship. Smooth invited me to give him a hand at basketball practice one day, and I accepted the invitation. The several coaches who worked with the team were all accepting and helpful. I waded back a little bit and just said a word or two here or there since I was the newest guest. My time after school was also limited by the fact that I was a newlywed and working on my master's degree while tackling my first full-time teaching assignment.

I attended as many games as I could. After one of them, I hung out at Smooth's crib. We talked about a lot—first basketball and work, but eventually we talked about more. Before we knew it, we were talking about life goals and business ideas. We tossed ideas back and forth, discussing things we thought might work, always wanted to do, and definitely had to do. He insisted that I *had* to write a book. I had always planned to do so and had notes and outlines for several future projects. I've always had book, movie, song, and music video ideas along with sitcoms and commercials stirring in my brain.

I appreciated the respect Smooth had for my writing and how avid he was that I make something of my talent. But by the next fall, I started teaching English at another high school and wouldn't see Smooth much anymore.

Smooth and I stayed in touch and hung out from time to time. He, his cousin Wayne, and I even got together and threw a small-scale party. Then suddenly it was on! An acquaintance of mine in the music business wanted a partner in bringing a concert to Memphis. I was to finance half the show, and the promoter was to provide the other half. After we paid the costs, we would split the proceeds. I immediately called Smooth to see what he thought of the idea. We researched the tour, got our sponsorship packages together, and were ready to go to work . . . but the deal fell through.

We were so deflated that we all went into hiding. Our phone calls to each other slowed, Smooth and I weren't hanging out as much, and I wasn't hearing from Wayne. That rollercoaster of events took a lot out of us. After a month or so in our separate stupors, we finally came back around. The phone calls picked back up, and we began to hang out a little again.

Then Smooth stunned me. He was considering not returning to his job at Overton in the fall. What shocked me more than that, however, was that he had not secured another job. I tried to be as objective as possible the next time Smooth and I talked—I don't believe in dissuading adults from making adult decisions. I was weary though. I felt like I was losing a dear friend. I did not plan to disown Smooth, but I had no idea where life would take him.

He said he had paid his bills in advance for a few months

and was going to make some things happen for himself. I knew he hated the structure of the school system, though he loved coaching, but I didn't think he would quit. I remember when he told me that his job at Overton was the first real job he had ever held in his life. He was groomed to play basketball as a child. He had played in the AAU and went to hoops camps and such rather than getting summer jobs.

I knew he wanted to be a promoter. I also knew that would involve making connections, which would take time and effort. This was my dilemma: I gain new friends seldomly due to my weariness of snakes and low tolerance for foolishness. So, I place a high value on the friendships that I do make. I didn't want to lose Smooth. I simply thought it was a bad move for him to leave his job without another job lined up, and I didn't want to see him in a bad position. But I didn't want to risk ruining our friendship by voicing my opinion, so I kept it to myself. He didn't ask for it; he had simply let me know what he had been thinking.

Ultimately, he did leave his job at Overton that year.

Then one day, less than a year later, I got a call.

Smooth: "Wha's up, Marc?

Me: "What it do, Smooth?"

Smooth: "Hey, me and Wayne throwin' a party next month. You want in?"

Me: "What I need?"

Smooth had started a marketing and promotions company, Moody Entertainment Inc. Memphis is a basketball city, and I think it's smart that Smooth had used his connections and popularity as a baller to aid his success as an entrepreneur.

I met Wayne Moody, who is vice president of Moody Entertainment, through Smooth. The two men are cousins but are like brothers. Wayne played college basketball at Christian Brothers University, where he not only hooped but also earned his bachelor's degree in marketing. The two make a good team.

The day before that first Moody Inc. event, which boasted more than 400 guests, Wayne and I were working inside the Gibson Guitar Lounge in downtown Memphis. In addition to promoting the party, we moved tables, sofas, and chairs like we were in the furniture business. I helped those guys however I could, although I wasn't a promoter.

I enjoyed working with them. Seeing young black men, who were my friends, follow their dreams and make things happen for themselves was reason enough for me to lend a hand. Too often, black men are seen as shiftless and uninspired, and that's not who we are.

Sponsorships followed, and events were scheduled clear through that summer and into the fall. By the end of that year, my guy had promoted ten events at venues ranging from the Bluefin, a local sushi bar that holds about 300 people, to the FedEx Forum in downtown Memphis, where the NBA's Memphis Grizzlies play.

Smooth was planning the Moody Inc. two-year anniversary party before I could blink. I'm pleased to see him accomplish his dreams. I also appreciate that he still asks for my opinion on matters despite his own personal success as a promoter. The mutual respect Smooth and I share is one of the strongest assets in our friendship. We admire each other. I respect his vision and ability to dream and pursue his dreams. I also admire his demeanor. We both know a lot of people in Memphis from simply being born and raised in the city. He knows way more people than I do because of the exposure he got as a Tigers basketball player. Then there are the people who know his face and want to know him. He cannot watch a basketball game, get a bite to eat, or have a drink without someone approaching him to say hello. The popularity isn't what I admire. I admire that he treats every last person who speaks to him with respect. It doesn't matter if the person is a millionaire Tigers program booster or a former elementary schoolmate from his neighborhood in South Memphis.

My old friends from Frayser and my family are proud of me for staying focused and finishing school. They are glad I'm not a statistic. I'm not a disgrace, but somehow a role model. Smooth told me the same thing and added that he is a college graduate because I'm a college graduate. I now get the feeling that I share my success as an educator, a scholar, and a person with more people than I realize. I certainly learned how to deal with popularity and have a "smooth" approach to life by hanging out with Marcus "Smooth" Moody.

THE TAKEAWAY

I took different lessons from each of the friends I introduced in this chapter. Disco taught me the importance of choosing my friends wisely through his example of ending up in jail as a felon who was addicted to drugs because of the crowd he chose. B-Dubb and my high school cross country and basketball teammates taught me the value of hard work and surrounding myself with people who motivate me to be my best. Diddy showed me that it's best to live in the present, not in the past. Ronnie showed me the importance of having a friendship where both friends anchor each other. Smooth pushed me to be my best and showed me the importance of making the most of my talents and managing success with humility.

Although my mother didn't handpick all my friends, she certainly shaped my thinking and helped me appreciate qualities that I should draw close to and qualities I should avoid. As you influence your students or children, it is not necessary to punish them—as Sporleder and Forbes advise in *The Trauma-Informed School*—to make them do as you want or, in the case of choosing friends, for who they choose to hang around. Instead, help them see how the friends they choose could be positively or negatively influencing their judgment. Trauma-informed mentorship teaches us that discipline is to teach, not to punish. Teach your students how to regulate themselves and surround themselves with friends who are also able to self-regulate.

CHAPTER 6

MAKE A WAY OUT OF NO WAY

"I'm just another black man caught up in this mix. I'm trying to make a dollar out of fifteen cents (a dime and a nickel)." That classic lyric was part of the hit Tupac Shakur single "I Get Around." And in his hit single "Keep Ya Head Up," Shakur rapped, "I'm tryin' to make a dollar out of fifteen cents. It's hard to be legit and still pay your rent." Then rapper Master P borrowed the same mantra and released a song called "Tryin' to Make a Dollar out of 15 Cents." Why was the theme so popular? What is the significance of "making a dollar out of fifteen cents"? It means you have to be prepared to make a way when there seems to be no way. As a child and young man who dealt with adverse childhood experiences, there were several instances where I felt like I had to make a way out of no way.

As you work with or raise children facing such challenges, keep in mind that finances—not necessarily just emotional challenges—may be impacting their ability to achieve goals. As you provide them trauma-informed guidance, learn more about these challenges and help them find solutions to overcome them. Consider the following stories.

MOMMA NEEDED A DOLLAR

The month I was to start college, I found a note from my mother pinned to the mirror on my bedroom dresser. I had come home after a day's labor as a produce employee for Piggly Wiggly to read:

"Marcus need
$1.00
Shirley."

Right around the time Momma left this note, the transmission would die in my car . . . right when I needed it to get to and from college for my freshman year. I didn't have the money to get it fixed.

I had to get to school some kind of way. So, here was the drill:

Momma didn't have a car, and Pop was out of pocket. So, I woke up at five a.m. to walk two miles from my parents' house to the bus stop. From there, I rode the bus to the downtown terminal. Then, I waited about twenty minutes for a transfer to the bus that would drop me off on campus around seven thirty. After that, I walked to my eight a.m. class. Once classes ended, it was back to the same bus stop, to the terminal again, a transfer from downtown, and then back home.

It had hurt me to realize that Momma didn't have a dollar to her name. After reading the note she left for me, I had noticed there were four quarters missing from my dresser. That almost brought me to tears then, and it still brings me near tears now to think that my dear, sweet, loving mother didn't have a dollar. I convinced myself that she wouldn't have to borrow money from anyone. I didn't know how I could ensure some security, but I knew going to school was a start. So, I trudged into the dark each morning to get there.

Those mornings were literally and figuratively dark. Each

morning I marched down that driveway, the sun hadn't risen and I was emotionally torn. Momma was getting progressively sicker. I was worried about my father's well-being, and I missed my brother Terry, who had moved out of the house, and hated that my younger brother, Greg, was experiencing so much pain and witnessing so much tragedy. My brother Marland, a once-shining academic light in our family, had been murdered two years before. So, I truly cherished the opportunity to attend college. In addition to all of this, Pop had dropped out of the University of Memphis about twenty years prior to me being admitted. He had married my mother after she got pregnant with Terry. Shortly after Terry was here, Momma had become pregnant with Marland. Subsequently, Pop had dropped out of college to work multiple jobs. My mother was a housewife. I knew that attending Memphis was a big deal to my father even if he wasn't around to give me a ride to class.

I try not to downplay the good works my father did, as some people have the tendency to do with their parents. I attribute much of my humble success to the fact that my father was in my life. We spent nights in the same house. Our mail was delivered to the same address. We watched old Westerns together. He taught me how to barbecue. He gave me the belt when I needed it. He demanded a paternity test when a girlfriend told me I had fathered her baby, which in honesty was another guy's baby. I have always yearned for my father's approval. So, I trudged out into the dark each morning.

It hurt Pop when Terry didn't return to college. It hurt, I think, even more when Marland reneged on an engineering scholarship to Memphis after being enrolled for a couple of years and dropped out too. I was only about thirteen when this happened, so the details are a little sketchy as to why. So, I kind of wanted to finish college for Marland. And so, I trudged into the dark each morning.

My mother had become accustomed to eating cereal and frozen vegetables. Greg was about thirteen and had no desire to eat bagged greens and Cheerios every day. I would buy fast food for him and me when I could. His favorite was a Big Mac meal with a Sprite. I wanted to help my little brother even more someday, and I wanted to set a good example for him. So, I trudged into the dark each morning.

That was my daily routine. Then I would do my homework on the bus ride. I've never been one to sit up and do nothing.

I saw all kinds of characters on that bus leaving my home in Frayser. There were the hardworking adults on the way to their daily grind. Their faces were often blank—blank with a wish, it seemed, a wish to rest more and work a little less. There were also those weird kinds of characters who didn't seem to be going anywhere in particular. I'm not one to pass judgment, though it was quite obvious to see that drugs had taken some people down a bad road. There were also students on the way to school. I wonder how many hung on in there and have a career to show for it now.

As for me, I was on the bus on my way to make the best of what I considered a screwed-up situation—screwed up because I had no real idea what I was doing in college. Yeah, I had earned a scholarship, but now what?

I thought I should join the school paper since I was on a journalism scholarship. So, I did. That idea led to the first failure of my college career. My writing was fine, but I had no idea how to apply Associated Press (AP) style to it. It embarrassed me to admit to my school newspaper colleagues that I did not know AP style, the standard mode of news communication. I didn't like editors butchering my work. So, I sought advice from Dr. Grusin, Tara, and Aimee, my mentors from the summer high school journalism program.

That year, those three women were my sun, moon, and stars.

They were compassionate and understood how badly I wanted to succeed with the newspaper and how seriously I took my writing. They told me that I could leave the paper and could always go back when I was more adjusted to college life and familiar with AP style.

My mentors made me feel like taking a break from *The Daily Helmsman* was okay, so I did. I did indeed return to that paper too. The next school year, I became a sports writer for the *Helmsman* and earned an internship at *The Commercial Appeal*, where I would intern in sports news. Later, I became the *Helmsman's* sports editor. I managed two writers, worked with copy editors, and was responsible for the layout of the sports section of the paper. Following that stint, I earned another sports writing internship, this time with the *Birmingham Post-Herald*.

As you can see, in the long run, I turned that failure at the school paper into a victory.

But back to freshman year. I caught the bus to school and bummed rides to work until I saved enough money to get my car fixed. This is the same year that I learned that I was supposedly to become a dad, news that would be disproven after a paternity test showed that I was not the father. This was also the same school year that my family's home was foreclosed upon.

Despite my personal and financial challenges, however, I kept finding a way out of no way. I stayed in school and kept pushing for my degree, bum car and all.

THE TAKEAWAY

There is no excuse powerful enough to stop your student from doing what they set their heart and mind to do. They simply need your support. They need you to be patient and encouraging. They need you to remember that their problems and setbacks are not about you. They need you to help them calm down and think clearly. That's what the instructors from my old summer journalism program did for me my freshman year at Memphis. They showed me that taking a break from working for the school paper did not spell defeat but would in fact help me succeed in school. They also showed me that walking away from the paper for a while did not mean I could not come back and write for it again. Of course, as you know, I did in fact return to the paper, which resulted in some great newspaper internships later.

Just like your students or children need your guidance, I needed the assistance of those instructors to help me organize my thoughts and manage my emotions in order to get and stay on the path to success. They did what Sporleder and Forbes advise in *The Trauma-Informed School*: They dropped their own point of reference—their personal mirrors—and listened to me and valued my voice. Without their guidance, I wonder where I would be today. Be the one who listens to and values the student's take. Ask how you can help. Explore the underlying issue behind the behavior.

CHAPTER 7

FORGIVE

"To err is human; to forgive, divine," wrote the English poet Alexander Pope. I agree with Pope because we all make mistakes. We are all imperfect. I also heard during a presentation on Kingian Nonviolent Conflict Resolution that, "Conflict is inevitable. Combat is a choice." In my view, the sooner we realize that life comes with problems, the sooner we can focus on moving past them. Oftentimes, this involves forgiving others. Over the years, that's what I've done. Consider this:

As much as I love my parents, I spent years traumatized from my childhood. I'm healing every day, though I like to think of myself as well adjusted. At the core of my healing has been the process of forgiving my parents for subjecting me to adult issues as a child; in addition to this is the realization that I have no room to hold any grudges because there are people who have chosen to forgive me for my own transgressions over the years. The following chapter shares stories involving my parents and how exercising forgiveness has allowed me to move past the pain of my past to live in the peace of my present. It's an important lesson to share with the children in your life who are battling ACEs.

MOMMA

Every day, Momma teaches me how to love a woman. Her schizophrenia makes her paranoid, which is a challenge to her and all those who care for her. The medicine she takes slows down many of her off-the-wall thoughts, but she moves slower than she used to. That makes her sad.

For about a decade, Momma went through a phase where she destroyed things. For example, in one day, Momma cut the names and numbers off my sports jerseys because she thought they bore secret messages that were meant to hurt her. I had saved money from my Fred's check to add to my growing jersey collection, and to see it decimated—and so quickly—tore me up.

I was nearly in tears when I asked Momma about what she had done. She explained that I didn't need all those numbers and letters on my clothes and said she thought she hadn't done anything wrong. I was sixteen at the time and didn't know that Momma was suffering from schizophrenia. I didn't know what schizophrenia was at all. I just knew that Momma was trippin'.

No one really knew how to react. Her destructive binges were only a fraction of the effects of her illness. She became detached from my brothers and me because she thought we were plotting to destroy her character. She accused us of wanting to have sex with her. We couldn't touch her or even go near her sometimes. No hugs, no pecks on the cheek, no nothing. Home felt like a prison when her condition reached its worst. Momma would interrogate us about the "scheme" she was so certain existed.

I never knew of a scheme to hurt my mother. My brothers and father said they never knew of it either. She insisted that we knew about the scheme and were in on it. For a long time, Momma also despised the color red. She destroyed or bleached all her red personal items and much of mine and Greg's too. She would talk about the color and sometimes spit on red things. Or she might spit after she said the word red. Once, Terry had insisted that his wife, who was then his girlfriend, change clothes before meeting Momma. She was wearing a red coat.

Momma would get angry at us when we said red had no special significance. She said we were brainwashed. Sometimes she would initiate the conversation by asking us what red meant. By the end of the conversation, she would be angry because she hadn't gotten to the bottom of the scheme that she was convinced existed. She would stare at people who wore the color in public, at the Kingdom Hall, in the grocery store, wherever. As tough as those times were for my brothers and me, they were nowhere nearly as tough for us as they were for my dear, sweet mother.

She lost a lot of friends. The severity of her condition was simply too much for many of them to take. She accused friends of twenty years or more of trying to hurt her by being in on the scheme. For several years, she used the words "scheme" and "plot" daily. Many of her friends wanted to help her but couldn't deal with the constant allegations Momma made against them. I could see their pain when they talked to us. The friends, with whom Momma used to go shopping, preach from door to door, and talk with on the phone, all seemed to distance themselves from her. I think they were as ignorant about schizophrenia as my brothers and I were. The difference was that they could walk away, but my brothers and I could not—would not.

Greg said that when he was about five years old, he heard our mother say she thought our car was bugged. About five years after that, her condition became obvious to almost all of our family and friends and became progressively worse over the ensuing years. Greg was Momma's riding buddy. At age eleven, he really had no choice. By this point, Marland was dead, Terry had moved, and I was between work and basketball practice. My baby brother witnessed a lot in his time alone with Momma.

I feel like Greg didn't get to know the Momma I knew. He

didn't know the woman who cooked delicious dinners every day and baked brownies, cookies, or cakes at least three days out of the week. He didn't know the woman whose smile lit up any room she walked into—the woman who could dance the four corners like nobody's business and loved to sing.

Many nights when I was a child, Momma baked brownies. The smell would overtake the entire house. Marland, Terry, and I would crowd around the oven anticipating the chocolate treats that waited inside it. The worst part was waiting on her brownies to cool. It was agonizing. They smelled so good! We were so hungry!

I loved the gooey ones! The chocolate chips would be melted in perfectly. I never wanted to eat from a paper towel or napkin because some of the chocolate would get stuck to the paper. I wanted to keep the brownie in my hand so I could lick my fingers and enjoy every last morsel.

I hardly eat sweets anymore. I just don't have the taste for them. I might try a slice of pecan pie or cheesecake every now and again, but I rarely eat brownies, cookies, or frosted cakes—Momma's specialties. I've never tasted a brownie better than hers. I don't know if I have a mental block about eating those particular pastries or what, but I just prefer not to eat them.

**

One of my mother's old friends, Dorothy, saw us at Walmart one day about ten years ago after Momma had just been released from the psychiatric ward. The help she received there, along with her medication, had made her comfortable to go out after years of isolating herself. Dorothy was nearly in tears as she spoke to my mother. Dorothy could tell something was different. Momma was calm, peaceful, and serene instead of wild-eyed and angry like she had been for the last decade or so.

Momma doesn't see many of her old friends from Memphis now that she has moved back to Tipton County where she grew up. It's still good to know that her friends will see someone like the Shirley they used to know if they see her. It's also good to give a good report when I see her old friends and they ask about her.

Her relationships with her own parents and siblings have improved too. Momma used to think her parents, Granny and Grampa, wanted her to be killed. She had also accused her brothers and sisters of being in on the scheme that she associated with the color red. Some of my mother's siblings, just like some of her old friends, distanced themselves from her. I can't imagine how I would feel if Terry or Greg said some of the things to me that Momma said to her sisters. It was hard for them to watch the sister they grew up with and loved, for lack of a better phrase, "lose it." She's improving though, slowly but surely from day to day.

She's more reasonable. She's less combative. She's even learning to trust again. She smiles now. She dances and even jokes from time to time. I love having my mother back.

Still, there are times when I have to try and stop her from worrying about daily problems, like not trusting maintenance workers when they come to check the heat or worrying about what she will do about paying her light bill if she doesn't receive her disability check. Worrying has become a part of Momma's personality. She has a list of things to worry about.

My brothers and I contribute to help her meet her financial needs. We try to assure her that we will be there for her when she needs us. Once, she was going on and on about a maintenance problem. I told her that my brothers and I would fix the problem as soon as we could, and we did. Joking with her, I asked what she would worry about next now that we had solved the issue. She responded with another task for my brothers and me to get busy working on before I could get the question out of my mouth.

POP

I figured I was good enough to play college basketball, and

since I loved the game so much, that was my plan. I was going to play for as long as I could, then I would become a firefighter, like Pop. Firefighting is a noble profession. Firemen save people's lives. Plus, I liked the idea of working ten days a month and being off duty for twenty days. My father was a lieutenant. He was working toward becoming a chief in the department and toward retirement. Unfortunately, however, Pop had to rebuild his entire life after becoming a product of his environment and screwing up.

It's humbling and scary when I compare my accomplishments and personality to my father's. My dad married young, and I did as well. His marriage failed, as did mine. He purchased his first house at age twenty-six, just like I did. He was a sharp, witty young man with the world as his oyster; people tell me that's me now. Now that I am an adult, we talk more often and openly than we ever did when I was a child, and Pop assures me of how proud he is of me and my brothers. He also cautions me when he sees the need.

Guidance and education start the separation of our spirits. Though we're both stubborn, my dad would never listen to reason unless it was on his side. Pop's mother, Madea, said of my father, "You can't tell him nothing." I'm an independent thinker, as is my dad, but I try to accept good advice when it's offered. Pop's dad died when my father was about twenty. His dad was a man of few words, and the two of them weren't very close. So, each time my father shares something with me I know that I'm getting more from him than he got from Grandpa John. Hopefully I will accept his guidance along with guidance from my family to keep me clear from hazardous mistakes.

Pop never finished college, though I wish he would even now. He was a college sophomore with a wife, two kids, and two jobs when he quit school. I, on the other hand, earned my bachelor's and master's degrees as a single man with no kids. When I told him I was considering becoming a doctoral candidate, he wasn't as supportive; he had mixed emotions. He said there is good money in teaching and maybe I should just stick to that. Southerners are often in favor of settling down when possible. The mentality is predominantly "set up and sit down." I explained to my father that my master's in teaching wouldn't dissolve and that I could always go back into the classroom if need be. I explained to him that I wanted to become a commodity, not just someone who can be hired and fired at whim with no consideration. Gaining as much education as possible won't guarantee success, I told him, but it will give me more leverage than most young black men raised and schooled in America have, especially the South.

**

Pop lived the American Dream, but he had two lives and two sides. In the scope of the American Dream, he was a young man from the country who married his high school sweetheart. He landed a well-paying job and provided for his family. He was well respected in the community. When he wore that firefighter's uniform, people in the neighborhood, the grocery store, or our school looked upon him with admiration.

His other life, though, was quite different. In the 'hood, it is commonly called the life of a "street nigga." In addition to fighting fires, his fights were with gambling, the pool table, and the card and dice games. Momma couldn't stand to be around most of his friends from the streets. She didn't approve of their language and the way they carried themselves. Pop told me how he got a thrill from breaking his cohorts on the dice. Some nights Pop would come home with thousands of dollars he had won in dice and card games.

One night, Pop turned on the lights in my and Greg's room in the wee hours of the morning and threw fistfuls of dollar bills on our dresser. We woke up happy and followed him into the den, where there was more money than my young eyes had ever seen. The next day, we arrived home from school to find a new washer and dryer in the kitchen. And suddenly, Pop was paying us dollars at a time to perform errands and chores that we normally performed for free. I've never celebrated Christmas in my life, but I guess those few days might have been what it feels like.

More often though, things were much more dismal after a night of my father's gambling. I recall countless nights when Pop would wake me up to say, "Your daddy done messed up." I could hear my mother begging him not to take the grocery money to gamble away.

While Pop harmed his fulfillment of the American Dream through gambling, I would fulfill the dream through my passion for education. I worked hard in college and earned degrees. From there, I became an educator. I enjoy working with young people and trying to instill the value of learning in them. A former chair of the journalism department said I spoke more to blacks on campus by simply walking around dressed in a shirt and tie, even if I never said a word, than he ever could. He was right. I am treated with respect when I dress up. Even in the grocery store, I have noticed that shoppers and employees not only acknowledge me but do so with smiles and address me as "sir." If I wear sweatpants or jeans in public, I'm often overlooked or even shunned.

I'm still a busybody like Pop though. I'm not big on gambling the way he was, but I have an interest in the stock market and trading. My understanding is rather superficial, but I plan to indulge more deeply as my understanding of the market deepens. That's my type of gambling. I don't have a problem with calculated risks—dice and cards, however, are not consistent enough unless you cheat, and people like to get violent over those type things where I'm from. Most importantly, I'm not a fan of cheating. Instead, I'm a fan of winning due to diligent effort and skill. In other words, I hustle.

I use the word hustle because I love what it means. Too often people associate a negative connotation with the word. They often think in terms of conning someone rather than the ideal of working feverishly and getting a move on it. Being born into the socioeconomic lower class and receiving a public school education in an urban neighborhood, you have got to work feverishly and get a move on it if you want to secure a life for your loved ones and yourself. Being a short guy who played a sport that is often ruled by the tallest players required hustle as well. I used to dive after loose balls and stalk taller and more athletic and talented players around the court until they didn't even want the ball, or by the time they got it they were too tired to make a move to the basket. That's hustle. That's why I was the shortest player on the team, but still on the team, because I worked feverishly and got a move on it. I hustled.

My dad smirks when I tell him I got his hustler spirit. He knows what I mean. I mean like Jay-Z, the rapper who owns his own clothing line, is president of his own record label, and part owner of an NBA franchise; Oprah, who does everything and owns more; Michael Jordan, the greatest basketball player of all time and the spokesman for Nike, Hanes, Gatorade, and who knows what else; Bill Gates, Microsoft's CEO; Will Smith, who has dedicated his time to empowering students through philanthropy; and Spike Lee, the filmmaker. The list goes on. They are all hustlers. They got a move on it.

Yes, I look up to my daddy. I was always crazy about him. I wanted my name to be Willie Jr. when I was little. Pop, aka Willie, loves to remind me of that. I would get up out of my bed and go sit up under my daddy on the nights I heard the TV. We would start watching *Shane* or *Cool Hand Luke* or a John Wayne movie together, and he would fall asleep within minutes. I rarely got to the end of the movies either. Momma would usually come to the living room and send me to bed.

I cherished those moments with my father. I think most children want to have an individual relationship with their parents, a relationship that's more than just being one of their kids. My being the middle child might have contributed to my desire to have "special time" with Pop. Yes, Pop and I developed a special relationship. Over the years, that relationship has continued to blossom. And the older I become, the more I appreciate Pop.

THE TAKEAWAY

Life is too precious and short to spend it holding grudges. No one is perfect, and we will make mistakes as long as we live. While it would not be wise to place yourself in harm's way by trusting people who don't deserve your trust, there is a difference between trusting someone who has earned your trust and trusting someone who has not. Forgiveness is a gift—it's a gift to the forgiver because you can be at peace without harboring anger and resentment, and it also a gift to the forgiven because you have an opportunity at redemption and reciprocity.

While there are countless arguments for forgiveness, remember that your student or child might not have done anything wrong. He or she could be an innocent victim with seemingly no one on their side. They could be crying on the inside. They could be in more pain than you could ever imagine. Keep this in mind when they make mistakes. They are still learning how to cope with being traumatized. Please forgive them freely and share with them why forgiving others can also release them from their own pain and suffering.

CHAPTER 8

EMBRACE DISAPPOINTMENT

I have never heard anyone say that every aspect of life is perfect. Everyone has been disappointed at one time or another. Sometimes we win; sometimes we lose. Sometimes things go our way; sometimes they don't. Sometimes we get what we want; sometimes we won't. This chapter is designed to help you teach your students or children how to make lemonade when life gives them lemons and how to view their disappointments as opportunities to produce better results than they first intended. There are no failures, only opportunities for growth.

BOOK TIME

"Well . . . here we go."

With those words, Trell asked me to start my book. We were hanging out at my friend Smooth's place one night, and I was reflecting on my life. I talked about some things I had seen and lived through—being a hospital baby, fighting a gastrointestinal condition that almost killed me at age fifteen, my brother's murder when I was sixteen, my dad's drug addiction, and my mom's battle with schizophrenia. It seemed like the worst in my life was behind me. Also, I had just lost my job and my then-wife had left me a few weeks earlier, the day before she graduated with her master's degree. I could feel the shift in my life that would ignite a new beginning.

Psychologist Daniel Levinson defined development in terms of constant cycles of steady periods and transitions. Steady periods exist in life—they could be a few years, maybe longer—and then there is a drastic change you have to adjust to, a transition, until things level off again. According to the theory, the pattern of steady periods and transitions never stop. My life has featured multiple transitions with seemingly few steady periods.

Things were stable for me until about age seven. My parents argued but seemed happily married. My older brothers teased me, and my little brother looked up to me. But when I was about seven, I noticed that some people seemed happy and others did not, some had a lot and others did not have much at all, and, for the first time, I realized that I could either please or displease those around me by my actions.

Things steadied after my revelation at age seven until about age fourteen. It was then that my mother's and my brother Marland's schizophrenic conditions—though we weren't aware that that's what they were suffering from—made life very difficult for not only Momma and Marland but the entire family and everyone that knew us.

Marland's murder in 1996 at age twenty-three was followed by my oldest brother Terry's self-isolation. Terry was a year older than Marland, and the two had been all but joined at the hip. Terry was more of an introvert, but he went into even more of a shell after his charismatic younger brother was murdered. After Marland's death, my father started to smoke crack cocaine. Momma's mental condition grew worse. I took flight to the streets, partying with friends. My brother Greg, age eleven, soaked it all in. Things were nowhere near steady for any of us. This period in my life was a beastlike barrage of transitions from bad to worse and worse than worse.

Things were steady for a hot second a few years after Marland's death when I landed an internship at *The Commercial Appeal*. That helped me gain direction and see a way out of poverty and hopelessness. Many people who knew me and my family might not have known my family's condition, but I assure you it is no exaggeration. We hid things well. My mom held up for a long time before breaking down. My father supported me, my brothers, and mother while gambling excessively and using drugs. I retreated to poetry and searched for love and affection by dating girl after girl while Terry left to clear his head and straighten his bearings. My dear brother Greg watched us all fall apart before his youthful eyes.

**

My internship cemented me as a credible writer and gave me a career goal. *The Commercial Appeal* wasn't a high school paper or a local poetry show. It was an established news fixture that chose me to work there to improve my skills and its newspaper. From there, I interned at another newspaper before graduating with a bachelor's of arts in journalism from the University of Memphis in 2003.

My life was seemingly coming together. My mom was coping with her illness, though still extremely paranoid and distrustful. My dad had beat crack and was working again, though, due to a forced resignation, he had lost the benefits he had earned for the seventeen years he had served with the Memphis Fire Department. Marland was gone but not forgotten. Terry was married and father to a beautiful daughter, though we weren't close friends after his departure following Marland's death. Greg was about to start college at Memphis, though I had no idea how much all the trauma he experienced as a child would follow him.

Me? I was all aces. The negative transitions were over. I had a college degree, my family was getting back on its feet, and I even found a girl to stick by me while I searched for a job after graduation. I was a grown man. I had conquered the world. What else was there to do besides get married and live happily ever after?

Evidently there was much more, and it started with work.

I didn't accept job offers outside Memphis because I felt my family needed me to stay home while we recovered from the tragedies we had all endured. So, I accepted a position at *The Commercial Appeal* writing obituaries as an editorial assistant. The job paid the bills but wasn't what I wanted to do with my talent. I didn't understand why many young journalists start their careers as editorial assistants or copy clerks or gophers. I thought I deserved to be a professional sports writer and was determined to take the first opportunity I could to be one.

I remember the phone call that led to my next transition. The man on the other end of the line said that he had contacted the University of Memphis in search of a reporter. He sought someone who knew sports and could write—someone who knew Memphis and was ready to be the star reporter for a local sports publication. He told me had been advised to find Marcus Matthews. This was just what I needed—an opportunity to show the city just how good I could write. It was an opportunity to show *The Commercial Appeal* editors that they were wrong for not making me a full-time reporter. Most importantly, it was a chance to do what I loved: write sports stories.

I left the *Appeal* to write for the *MidSouth Youth Sports Authority*. That job lasted about four months before the paper folded and the owner filed for bankruptcy.

At the time, I was living with my father's mother, Madea. She had all but begged me not to quit my job at the *Appeal*. I can still hear her sweet, concerned voice: "That paper been 'round a long time, Marcus. Das a good job! You got benefits."

Still, the sweet lady understood my desire to be a writer. "But you're young, son," she reminded me. "And people can take chances when they young."

I had talked to my mentor Otis Sanford, the *Appeal's* deputy managing editor, too. Mr. Sanford was my boss' boss and had been one of my mentors since my high school journalism days. He had let me know the decision to leave was mine to make, but he made me aware that most new businesses, especially news publications, fail within the first couple of years. I had also spoken to the woman who recruited me out of high school and introduced me to journalism, Dr. Elinor Grusin. She had advised me to stay at the *Appeal* as well.

I wanted to sue the publisher once the paper folded, but there was nothing I could do. Things were not steady for me. I was an unemployed college graduate living with my grandmother.

Not long after my short-lived job, I started substitute teaching for the Tipton County Schools (TCS). I planned to do that until I landed a better job and found my way again. Fortunately, it didn't take long for me to realize that I liked teaching. With little convincing from my cousin Ricky, who was also associate superintendent for TCS, the following fall I started classes in pursuit of a master's degree in the art of teaching. I was enrolled in August and accepted a position with the Memphis City Schools system as an English teacher a few months later.

I also found time to get married, and marriage was rough. Neither of us was prepared to center our lives on another person. My wife was the offspring of an independent single mother, and my papa was a rolling stone.

I didn't blame our parents' actions and lifestyles for that marriage's failure, but we didn't receive proper marriage training. Growing up, we hadn't seen examples of happily married people from day to day. We saw our loving parents doing what they could to make sure we could survive in a cold world. She cited that she had inherited her mom's independent spirit, while I cited that my father's domineering spirit lived in me. It wasn't a good combination.

Three years after our marriage, she left me. A month later, I found out that my teaching license would not be renewed for the upcoming school year because of a test and a class I had not yet taken. Unemployed and in emotional shambles, I was shaken but not rattled. I had been in tougher pickles before.

That brings us back to Smooth's crib. I was talking things through with my friend. I only told Greg and Smooth that my license could not be renewed. I'd had to tell someone, but I didn't want my parents or Terry to worry about me. Greg was the closest person to me, and Smooth knew I could pull a rabbit out of a thimble. His childhood friend Trell knew I wasn't teaching and that my ex and I had separated. After listening intently to me and Smooth share thoughts for a while, Trell interjected, "Sounds like book time to me!"

He was right. He knew about my journalism background, and Smooth had told his family and friends that I was a writer when he introduced me. I made a few agreeable comments about writing a memoir, but there was no conviction. Trell could sense it and said again, "Sounds like book time to me!"

Then he said to me, "Just do me one favor. Start if off, 'Well (as he mimicked typing motions) . . . here we go.' "

After that conversation, I started working on my autobiography. The book has not yet been released. Instead, in 2010, I released a book called *I Am Not the Father*, which detailed my journey proving that I was not the father of a former girlfriend's baby. Then the next year I released my second book, *Runners*, intended to inspire children to run toward their dreams.

I appreciate the motivation I got from Trell though. I always planned to tell the story of my life. I had just been waiting on the right moment. *Urban ACEs* is the current result, though a longer book with more of my life stories is in the making. And even though I didn't begin this book as Trell had asked, I took his advice to embrace my disappointment by beginning a new facet of my literary journey that has brought us all to this point. So . . . well . . . here we go.

TERRY

When I was growing up, my brothers and I would spend our summers playing basketball in the gym at Westside High. The school's then-athletic director, Paulette Moore, and football coach Richard Horner would chaperone. My brothers and the older guys would run five-on-five on the full court on the main floor, while us youngsters played 21, two-on-two, or three-on-three on the side courts. Sodas cost fifty cents.

One afternoon at the gym, I bought a drink with a dollar and put my fifty cents in change in my pocket. As I was playing a game of 21, my change flew out of my pocket and onto a side court. A bully from the apartments across the street stepped on both of my quarters. I jumped to shoot the basketball and heard change jingle on the floor. Then I saw Ced's feet stomp the ground. I was about ten. Ced was about thirteen.

I knew he had stepped on my money, and I wanted it back. He refused to lift his foot from the floor. I told him to give me my money, and he told me he didn't have it. He threatened to kick me when I went to pull his leg from the floor. We argued for a few minutes about the two quarters, and he turned to walk away. I followed him out of the gym because I knew he was walking away with my money.

I followed that boy across the street to the apartments where he lived. He argued with me outside, picked something up, and threatened to hit me. I didn't cower. Suddenly, Terry showed up out of nowhere. He asked me why I had left the gym and what

I was doing at the apartments. I pointed to the other kid and said he took my money. Terry told Ced to give it back to me. Ced insisted that he did not have it.

Terry was about seventeen and wasn't going to argue with me or the other kid. He told Ced I was too little for him to pick on and then told me to get back over to the gym. My big brother roasted me pretty good on the walk back over there. He said I'd had no business leaving and that something bad could have happened to me in those apartments. It was the first time I recall Terry ever putting me in line.

Basketball was always our common denominator aside from sharing the same bloodline. Many of my stories regarding Terry involve basketball in some way.

I remember when my aunts played in an informal league in Tipton County. I don't think they had jerseys. They invited me and my brothers out to join them. Terry told me to sit in the bleachers and watch while he joined the team and played. I remember that clearly. He said no when I asked if I could sit on the bench with the players, but my aunts overheard and said it was okay for me to do so.

So, I disobeyed my big brother. I left the stands and took a seat on the bench while my brother was checked into the game. He was angry when he got subbed out and returned to the sideline to see me sitting on the bench. He then told me not to expect to ride with him anywhere else anytime soon, and he meant it. I tried to explain that my aunts said it was fine for me to sit there. He told me that I left the house with him and that he was the person I should have listened to while I was in his care. He also told me to see if my aunts would come pick me up to play next time because I wouldn't be riding with him. He was right.

Often, Terry is right. I have to grant him that. He might not be the most outgoing person or the life of any party, but he usually knows what he's talking about when he decides to speak his mind.

I look up to that guy, and I miss him. These days, there's an awkward feeling when we see each other at my grandparents' house because he won't speak to me. Neither will his wife or daughter. Fellowshipping with me is off-limits unless I confess my sins to the Jehovah's Witnesses and write a letter for reinstatement to their organization—an organization I left some time ago. In the meantime, Terry, his family, my mother, and several aunts and cousins don't acknowledge me at all—even when we're in the same house—unless there is a business- or health-related concern.

I have to grow from the disappointment of being rejected by several members of my own family. I should have thought longer and done more research before I decided to join their religion—and leave their religion. Had I not become baptized as a Jehovah's Witness, I would still be able to hug and fellowship with my entire family. As a result, I tell my family members how I feel as much as possible, whether they will respond in turn or not. I love harder, and I'm glad that I do. I never want anyone in my family to ever question my love for them. I love them all. Even those who don't speak to me.

THE TAKEAWAY

The world keeps spinning and time keeps ticking when something unfortunate happens. Life will present disappointments. There is a time for remorse and sadness, but there is also a time to move on as best you can. I've been hurt over and over—from losing my brother to death, from losing another brother to a religious difference, from a failed marriage, from foiled career opportunities and more. When you are mentoring your students, learn their stories. As Sporleder and Forbes write in *The Trauma-Informed School*, "Be the one who listens and values the student's voice." Try to understand what personal disappointments and ups and downs they're managing as you implement your trauma-informed mentorship. Doing so will allow you to strategically teach them to use their disappointments as opportunities to make themselves stronger, wiser, and better prepared for life's challenges. This can help them keep their heads up in the midst of adversity and still achieve their goals.

CHAPTER 9

KEEP YOUR BALANCE

In this chapter, I reflect on the loss of my brother Marland. It was difficult to keep my balance after his death. I was sad, hurt, angry, lost, and confused. When your students are struggling with these emotions, you can help them make it through by lending a listening ear, offering supportive words, and giving them space to grieve and room to be imperfect.

MANAGING THROUGH TRAGEDY

On Friday nights, my brothers and I played basketball together. When we won, we high-fived and slapped butts, and verbal praise flowed like the water Langston Hughes spoke of in the epic "A Negro Speaks of Rivers" poem. When we lost, we pointed fingers, got upset, and nearly came to blows about the game we loved. Still, we went home together regardless of the outcome of the game.

One night was very different. Terry and Greg and I had gone to play without Marland, the second oldest of us.

Marland had been acting weird the last few years. It was hard to hang around him. He would say people were trying to hurt him. He staunchly believed there was an all-out conspiracy to assassinate his faith and character along with the faith and character of those close to him.

I don't remember if we invited Marland to go along with us that night. On the drive home from the court, Terry said that he wished Marland would be like he used to be and spend more time with us. I answered that I didn't care if he hooped with us or not. I said as long as we knew he was okay it was cool. We held that conversation on September 13, 1996. Later that night while listening to the radio, we found out that rapper Tupac Shakur had been murdered. The news was sobering because Tupac seemed so real to me although I had never met him. I felt like I had lost a friend.

The next day, I went to work. As I type, I still haven't recovered from the news I received after I arrived home from my job that day.

Terry came over. It was a Saturday. This was odd because we mostly saw him on Fridays for basketball. Terry brought the news that his little brother, my big brother Marland, was dead.

He said that my dear, sweet brother's wallet had him listed as the next of kin and that he had been contacted earlier that day to identify Marland's body. Terry said that he traveled to Helena, Arkansas, where Marland had washed ashore from the Mississippi River. From there, Terry had visited the coroner and identified his little brother. Water had so inflated and deformed Marland that Terry could only identify him by his clothes and a ring on his finger.

The news devastated the family. Terry, who was twenty-four, became even more of an introvert than he had already been. My henlike mother, who like Marland had also been behaving mysteriously, became an emotional wreck. My father, the lieutenant with the city fire department, disciplinarian, and provider who also suffered from alcoholism, grew more out of touch with the family than his habits and responsibilities had already taken him. Greg was only eleven. Me . . . I was flabbergasted. I was sixteen and simply bowled over by the fact that my brother was dead.

No one in the family was up to the responsibility of planning Marland's funeral, but it had to be done. My mom's sister Doris was a tremendous aid in assuring my brother's death would be addressed in the respectful and dignified manner it deserved. She and I worked feverishly to guarantee that things would take place decently and by arrangement. I will always love her for that. Other family members helped too. There was a lot to be done. Planning Marland's funeral and the accompanying activities was among the first of many challenges I would face.

In the midst of all of this, I didn't miss school. My cross country coach, Philip Butler, told me I didn't have to practice if I didn't feel up to it. Yet I didn't miss a day of practice or a meet that season. But it had been important to know that Coach Butler would give me the room to mourn if I needed it. However, I thought that the best thing for me to do was to continue to live as normally as possible. More than a decade after Marland's death, Daniel Coleman, one of my friends, told me that I was one of the strongest people he knew based on the way I dealt with my brother's passing.

I mourned though. I was hurt. I still hurt, and I still miss Marland. But I knew back then that somebody had to be strong for the family. Somebody had to say that things would be alright. There is a special comforting power in hearing, "It's gonna be alright."

** **

Everybody dealt with Marland's death differently. No two people mourn exactly the same.

I had never seen my father cry before Marland died. But cry he did.

Terry cried the night he brought the news of Marland's death. Momma cried throughout the period of Marland's death until the funeral and on afterward.

Terry drove Greg and me from Memphis to Madea's, where all the family—parents, brothers, cousins, uncles, aunts, everybody—had gathered the morning of the funeral. Upon greeting everyone and seeing faces we had not seen in years, we all cheered up. Everyone was hugging, smiling, and laughing almost as though we were there for a family reunion. In the blink of an eye, however, the mood changed. A long green limousine swung a slow smooth right turn onto Peeler Road. It was the first car in the funeral procession.

A hush came over the entire party like my brother was being murdered all over again, but right in front of our eyes this time. Pop's eyes filled with tears. He started crying. I put my arms around him, and he leaned on my shoulder. Terry and Pop's youngest brother, Ramell (Uncle Ray), were there to comfort my dad as well. I didn't cry. My dad needed me, and it seemed like the whole family started crying after Pop. Terry, Uncle Ray, everybody was crying. Those who were slightly teary comforted those who were breaking down.

At the funeral, I read a poem I had written about my dearly departed brother. Uncle Ray, a pall bearer, sat in the front row. We were eye to eye as he cried while I read the poem. There were more tears from many others after the funeral and at the burial; still no tears from me though. I had to facilitate. The facilitator has always been one of my roles, in basketball, with friends, wherever.

The burial was tough, more tears and wailing. After my brother was placed in the ground, onlookers headed to the repast. It was over. I could feel that it was over. Marland had died. Everybody grieved. My aunt and I had facilitated the ceremony. The funeral was done. Marland's body was in the ground, and now it was time to eat.

Outdone by the finality of the circumstances, I gave in. I got down on my knees to look at the casket in the ground, still uncovered, and I bawled like a baby with no bottle. I sniveled and sobbed and slobbed. I snotted and heaved deep until it was out of me. It had to be that way. Marland's funeral had had to be taken care of first. Everything had had to be facilitated, then I could let go. Then I could begin to release some of the grief and pain I still suffer from to this day.

THE TAKEAWAY

Trauma-informed mentorship allows you to help your students keep their balance when their worlds are turned inside out and upside down. Dropping your personal mirror and not being offensive if the child acts out is crucial. If you as the adult get sidetracked or bent out of shape because your traumatized student has acted out, no one wins. Your student needs you to be the mature adult you are and de-escalate the situation, not make it worse by alienating, blaming, downing, humiliating, or yelling at them. Your student needs you to help them get back up when they get knocked down.

In my case, coaches and other adults advised me that I could take time away from practice and extra time to complete assignments—things I did not take them up on, but that I appreciated being offered. Just knowing that they were open to giving me room to grieve—a sign of their respect for me and empathy for my situation—helped me stay focused in the classroom and in sports from day to day. It is up to you to remain resolute yet caring when your students or children face challenging situations. Show them how they can do it too!

CHAPTER 10

BE YOUR BROTHERS' AND SISTERS' KEEPER

My mother gave birth to four sons, but I only spend time with one of my brothers. According to their religion, as I mentioned previously, my mom and Terry are not allowed to fellowship with me because I am no longer a member of the Jehovah's Witnesses. So, sometimes it feels like Greg is my only brother. He has been my best and closest friend for decades. Still, no matter where my other brothers are—dead, estranged, or otherwise—I will always care about and love them. I am my brothers' keeper, and you, as part of the human race, are your brothers'—and sisters'—keeper too.

ROBERT COLE

When Junior asked me to be a pall bearer at his mother's funeral, I was saddened, shocked, and honored. I was saddened because one of my best friends had lost his mother, which had devastated him. His voice trembled. I could hear how scattered and confused he was through the phone. I was sad because I knew he would mourn the loss of his mother for years to come.

I was shocked because her death came as such a surprise. In fact, phone calls from Robert Lekevin Cole always surprised me. Junior, my nickname for Robert, had moved from Memphis to Nashville and didn't call me when he visited his mother in the months before she died of cancer. He never even told me she had cancer. That's Junior.

Very few people on this earth internalize their feelings as well as Junior does. There were times, as undergraduate students at Memphis, that he would not speak. He literally would not open his mouth. Not to me, any of his other friends, or anyone else. He might go silent for minutes, maybe hours. That's just Junior.

Junior and I met at a frat party at Memphis. The two of us were there because we were interested in joining the fraternity. We may have been the only guys at the party who weren't already in the frat. We talked to each other all night.

By the time the party ended, we were friends. Soon, either I was calling him or he was calling me about an event that a fraternity or sorority was throwing. We attended a lot of them together. Junior was my first college friend.

He and I were an interesting fit. He was quiet. I was loud. I liked to dance. Junior stood against the wall. I wore oversized T-shirts and jeans. Junior wore polo shirts tucked into his slacks. We balanced out each other's personalities.

My friend was an only child. I was raised with three brothers. After stopping by his dorm room one night, I began to understand why that was significant.

That night, he was ironing an outfit in his room. I asked him where he was going, and he said he was going to a club by himself. "Why didn't you tell me?" I asked with confusion. Junior shrugged and said he didn't think about telling anyone and that he had just felt like going.

Later, I realized that he was accustomed to doing things by himself. I always admired that about him and thought it took a strong person to do that. He could go to a movie by himself or sit in a restaurant alone. I had never done any of those things. I guess Junior, being an only child, found it easy to do things on his own without thinking about a second party.

My parents used to force my older brothers to carry me along with them when I was young. They hated it too. I cramped their style. Nonetheless, I can hear Momma saying, "Take your brother witcha," as Marland and Terry were headed up to Westside Park to hoop or to a friend's house. The situation was much the same when Greg got old enough to tag along with me.

Junior and I became brothers in a sense as well. Though he sometimes needed his space, and I gave it to him, we continued to tag along with each other. We were there for each other in important times and shared deep experiences. Years later, Junior not only invited me to be a part of his wedding, but he asked me to be his best man. I was honored. Junior taught me that being a friend, a best friend, a brother's keeper, is not about having all the same interests or doing everything the same way— or doing things together all of the time. Being a friend is about caring for your friend.

MARLAND

I remember going to a popular store in town with my mom and brothers when I was a little boy. I must have been about four years old because I don't remember Greg taking the trip. It was sprinkling outside. My mother gave me a dollar so I could buy something. I distinctly remember her tucking that dollar as deep into my pant pocket as it could go before we left home and telling me to leave it in there until we got in the store.

I didn't listen. I yanked that dollar from my pocket as soon as I thought she wasn't paying attention. The rain was coming down hard by the time she parked in front of the store. Momma gave Marland and Terry instructions to move quickly and out of the rain, and she took me by the hand so we could hurry inside. I put my dollar back in my pocket before Momma could whisk me out of the car. As we were shaking off the rain before we went into the store, I checked for my dollar. It was gone.

I started to cry. I knew I had screwed up. Momma had clearly told me to leave that dollar in my pocket until we got in the store, but I was hardheaded. When she asked why I was crying, I told her that I had lost my money. She and my brothers looked around the immediate area for a minute or two, but there was no dollar in sight. My four-year-old world was devastated until Marland spoke up. My big brother, who was eleven, volunteered to go back into the rain to help me find my money. We retraced our route from the store back to the car and didn't find anything. I started to cry again as we got close to the store entrance because I knew my dollar was gone and that Momma was not going to give me another one.

I don't remember my first day of kindergarten or the first bucket I made playing basketball, but I vividly remember that day searching for that dollar in the parking lot. Standing there in the rain, in one motion, Marland took a dollar from his pocket, balled it up, and threw it to the ground. I saw him do it. He pointed to it and told me to look. I smiled bigger than a kid who has found two toys in his Happy Meal instead of just one. I reached down and snatched up the dollar, and we met back up with our family and walked into the store.

That's what I remember about my brother. He was quick on his feet. He was a loving young man.

It never seemed fair to me that he was murdered. I realize he is dead, but I still don't want to accept it. Sometimes when I'm confused, I ask myself what Marland would want me to do. I wonder what he would be doing if he were still on this earth. Not a single day passes without me thinking about him in some shape, form, or fashion. When I make new acquaintances, I always tell them that I have three siblings. This gives me a chance to talk about Marland.

THE TAKEAWAY

As I stated at the start of this chapter, all of us, as members of the human race, are our brothers' and sisters' keepers. What we have and who we have are each other. Our daughters and sons, nieces and nephews, adopted and foster children, brothers and sisters, grandchildren, students, and future generations need us. It starts at home, and it takes off from there. The millions of children in the world who have been traumatized, who are braving through adverse childhood experiences daily, need you. It does not matter how different your experience is from their experience, whether you're eight years older or eighty years older than them, a blood relative or a schoolteacher. You can be as different as Junior and I were, but like we were there for each other, you can be there for your child or student. Like Marland showed creativity and caring toward me in that incident with the lost dollar—not condescension or impatience—you can do the same for a struggling child.

Children need you to exercise your human and professional responsibility to provide trauma-informed care and mentorship to help them realize their potential and become good citizens. They also need you to help them self-actualize to a point where they become advocates and mentors. The load is heavy, but the rewards are worthwhile.

CLOSING WORDS

While I am living a fulfilling existence and walking in my purpose each day, my story is by no means the be-all and end-all prototype of successfully overcoming adverse childhood experiences. I shared life anecdotes to provide examples that illustrate how children can overcome ACEs and how influential adults such as parents, teachers, guardians, family members, and school administrators can help them.

I would like for parents, teachers, and other adults to use this book as a starting point to help children achieve success despite struggling with ACEs. Helping the student or your child *develop a strong work ethic, choose battles wisely, develop their talents, keep their best foot forward, find good friends, make a way out of no way, forgive, embrace disappointment, keep their balance,* and *be their brothers' and sisters' keeper* is a great place to start.

Urban ACEs is a jumping off point for continued dialogue to support students dealing with ACEs. There is much more to learn and much more to discuss—particularly, how do we academically empower students dealing with adverse childhood experiences? I look forward to being a part of healthy, serious, and constructive conversations linked to the plight of students dealing with ACEs. In the meantime, I will continue to lend myself to the cause of equity and success for all people the best way I know how.

ABOUT THE AUTHOR

Dr. M. L. Matthews is an author, speaker, producer, and doctor of education. He overcame a tumultuous childhood in Memphis to thrive in the Lionel Linder Journalism Camp, a high school outreach program that turned his life around. Cosponsored, among others, by the University of Memphis and Memphis City Schools, he received one of only two college journalism scholarships offered by the program and enrolled in the University of Memphis.

As an undergraduate, Matthews worked as a reporter and editor for his campus newspaper and interned for the *Birmingham Post-Herald*, the Associated Press, *The Commercial Appeal*, and the NBA's Memphis Grizzlies. After earning his bachelor's degree in journalism, he taught English, speech, contemporary issues, and African-American literature in Memphis City Schools. He went on to receive a master's in the art of teaching and a doctorate in higher and adult education at Memphis, where he coordinated the program that helped send him through college.

Recently, Matthews served as the dean at a Memphis middle school, where he helped facilitate a 26 percent reduction in out-of-school suspensions in one school year, from 228 suspended students to 168. Currently, he is the executive director of the Matthews-Fayne Foundation, a nonprofit group that supports education initiatives for urban youth. The foundation focuses on supporting students with adverse childhood experiences, promoting access and retention in higher education for minority, underprivileged, and at-risk students, and building partnerships between corporations and educational institutions.

His first book, *I Am Not the Father: Narratives of Men Falsely Accused of Paternity*, and the namesake documentary that aired on cable television were featured on the *Maury Show* in 2012. His children's book, *Runners*, was released in 2011.

CPSIA information can be obtained
at www.ICGtesting.com
Printed in the USA
LVHW051614170720
660992LV00002B/267

9 781633 939851